Plain Legal Writing: Do It

Plain Legal Writing: Do It

By Wayne Schiess

Copyright © 2019 Wayne Schiess
All rights reserved.

For Sarah, Cory, Anna, Davis, Noah, and Logan.

Table of Contents

The Audience for Plain Legal Writing 1

What Is Plain English? 5

A Plain-English Drafting Process 21

Designing Plain Legal Documents 31

Drafting Conventions & Plain English 43

Organization & Signposts 57

Plain Letters & Email 69

Plain-English Words 79

Plain-English Sentences 91

Testing Your Plain-English Drafts 107

Using Readability Tests 117

Before and After 125

Plain Legal Writing: Do It

The Audience for Plain Legal Writing

You're not writing for other lawyers.

Picture a nonlawyer reader, baffled or exasperated by legalese. Think of that person when you write plain-English legal documents for nonlawyers.

Too many legal documents intended for nonlawyers are dense, archaic, and unnecessarily complex. A big part of the problem is that these documents contain traditional legalese: jargon, terms of art, long sentences, and complicated syntax. What's more, these documents sometimes contain grammar mistakes or substantive law mistakes, both of which are harder to spot and fix because the text is written in traditional legalese. Ultimately, these documents fail in their essential purpose: to communicate binding legal content to a nonlegal reader.

We can do better, and that's my goal: to teach you how to convey binding legal content, in plain English, to nonlawyers.

The audience for plain legal writing

In this book, the focus is on the audience of nonlawyers. Keep that in mind. Picture an elderly nonlawyer relative if you have to, but break the habit of writing for the general public the way you write for other lawyers. Remember, the nonlawyers reading your text have widely varying levels of education, from Ph.D.s to grade-school educations. For so wide an audience, aim a bit low. I often

2 Plain Legal Writing: Do It

aim for a tenth-grade reading level, and when the context is particularly important, I try to go even lower. I once revised a set of jury instructions to a seventh-grade level.

I aim below the likely reading level because that helps the audience. You see, nonlawyers are often not at their best when they're reading legal documents. They read under stress, with negative emotion, and with preconceived ideas and confusion. They read in fear. Here's a taste of what it's like for them:

> RELEASE
>
> KNOW ALL MEN BY THESE PRESENTS, that I/we Linda Smith residing at 1000 Amber Lane, Emmett, ID, the undersigned, First Party, for and in consideration of the sum of FIVE THOUSAND AND NO/100 Dollars ($5,000.00) to me/us in hand paid by Real Insurance, Inc. and John James, Second Party, the receipt of which is hereby acknowledge, I/we being of lawful age, for myself/ourselves, my/our heirs, administrators, executors, successors and assigns hereby remise, release, acquit and forever discharge the said Second Party, his/her, their, and each of their heirs, executors, administrators, successors, and assigns and any and all other persons, partnerships, associations, and/or corporations, whether herein named or referred to or not, of and from any and every claim, demand, right, or cause of action of whatever kind and nature, either in law or equity, especially liability arising from an accident which occurred on or about 08/11/2005 at or near the following location INTERSTATE 1, ANYTOWN, USA for which I/we have claimed the said Second Party to be legally liable, but this release shall not be construed as an admission of liability.

The woman who received this and forwarded it to me was an English teacher with a master's degree, and I expected a complaint about the writing or a critique of the word usage or even the typos. But she didn't point out how badly written it was or complain that it contained typographical errors and archaic legalisms. No. What she asked was, "Should I sign this? What does it mean?" There was confusion and frustration. Even for an English teacher, the legal language was overwhelming.

With this kind of legal text, the "baffle factor" is high. Surely anyone reading it—even a lawyer—can see that. So why do we write that kind of dense legalese for nonlegal readers?

Why we don't write well for nonlawyers

Maybe we haven't been taught. I surely wasn't taught the skill of writing about legal subjects in plain English in law school—almost no lawyers were. And even today, I teach plain-English transactional drafting only to the small percentage of law students who take my advanced courses.

Maybe we're stuck in the habit of "writing like a lawyer," which usually means our writing is excessively formal. One of the main things I strive to get across in my courses and will strive to get across in this book is that to adapt to the nonlegal audience, you must change your outlook completely. You must think about communicating the ideas as clearly and simply as you can. You must elevate the importance of the expression of the ideas to the same level as the importance of the substance of the ideas.

Maybe we're afraid of sounding unsophisticated. To communicate with nonlegal readers, you'll need to write in a voice that is closer to spoken English, or what we might call a colloquial tone. For nonlawyers, a colloquial tone is not only good; it's also necessary. It might be foreign to you now, but you can learn. You can learn to invite the reader in. You can abandon the fear that it won't sound legal. You can abandon the approach of writing to impress. This book will teach you how. After all, what you're writing is important stuff.

The documents nonlawyers need to read

Many, many legal documents are intended for the nonlegal audience. Here are just a few examples of documents that nonlawyers should be able to read and understand:

Apartment leases
Consumer regulations
Credit-card agreements
Employee manuals and handbooks

4 Plain Legal Writing: Do It

    Homeowner's association bylaws
    Insurance policies
    Jury instructions
    Opinion or advice letters
    Public notices
    Releases
    Software licenses and user agreements
    Website disclaimers
    Wills

And more. The list would include any legal content for nonlawyers, which generally means content related to consumer transactions and communication between people and their government. These documents affect rights and liabilities and have as their primary intended audience the general public—nonlawyers.

Do you write any of those kinds of documents? If so, this book is for you.

Just for fun, these stories capture the way I think about plain-English writing.

A woman approached the elevator in a fancy hotel and asked the attendant, "Is this elevator ascending or descending?"

"I'm sorry, ma'am," he replied, "but you'll have to ask at the front desk about that." Then he called out, "Going up!"

It's a nice story with a simple message: big words don't always get the message across, so use language your audience can understand. Imagine my pleasure to have been present when a similar incident occurred. I was at a meeting for a charity and we were planning a meeting of potential donors. One committee member addressed the person in charge:

"For the meeting, do you require assistance in providing enhanced capacity?"

"I don't know about that, but we need your help to set up more chairs."

That's what this book is about. No, not chairs or meetings, but communicating plainly, so people can understand.

What Is Plain English?

Get informed and begin practicing the principles of plain English.

I stated in the Introduction that the goal of this book is to teach you how to write binding legal text so nonlawyers can read and understand it. But what does it mean to write so nonlawyers can understand? It means to write in plain English. So what is plain English? Defining plain English is deceptively simple and yet complex. I take a stab at defining it here, with nine plain-English principles. Then I recommend some excellent sources for further study. Finally, I debunk some common myths about plain English.

Before I begin, a caution about the word "plain": don't let it lead you to believe that plain English is dull, drab, or boring. Rather, "plain English" simply means a form of English that is appropriate to its intended audience. It is a form of English that uses every tool at its disposal to make text clear, simple, and direct. But even though plain-English experts have been explaining that for many years, the concept of plain English is still sometimes criticized: "[Plain language] has a bad name among some lawyers. This is usually because they don't understand enough about it to judge it properly."[1]

Yes, the main criticisms of plain English often come from the uninformed. You won't be one of them. Below are nine key

---

1. Michèle M. Asprey, *Plain Language for Lawyers* 11 (3d ed. 2003).

6 Plain Legal Writing: Do It

principles for preparing legal documents in plain English in the order in which they appear in this book.

The plain-English writing principles in this book

Know and write for the nonlegal audience (Introduction)

To communicate binding legal text effectively, you must be aware of the needs and limitations of the intended audience. To some extent you must forget you're a lawyer. Instead, you must think carefully about how to explain complex legal subjects in everyday language.

Master your forms—and develop a process for plain-English writing (Chapter 1)

Much incomprehensible legal writing is handed down from previous documents, whether you prefer to call them forms, templates, guides, or precedents. Using forms is, of course, necessary for legal practice. Retaining the bad legal writing in the forms is not. You need a reliable, step-by-step process for converting legalese into plain English.

Design readable text: manage type and lines; design accessible documents; use summaries, headings, and numbering (Chapter 3)

No one practicing law is using a typewriter, so everyone preparing documents for nonlawyers should take advantage of modern document-design principles. These principles will enhance the accessibility and readability of legal documents.

Use consistent, modern writing and drafting conventions (Chapter 4)

Just because we're writing in plain English doesn't mean we can afford to be sloppy, inconsistent, and hasty. Learn and practice the modern rules of legal-drafting language. These principles apply to traditional legal drafting as well as to plain-English legal drafting.

Plan and execute a sensible organization with summaries, headings, numbering, and connected paragraphs (Chapters 4, 5, and 6)

Think about what's important to the nonlegal reader and order your document accordingly. Think about the way typical readers use a document, then make it easy for them to skim your document, skip around in your document, and get key information quickly and easily.

Test documents on readers (Chapter 7)

You probably spent years in law school and law practice conditioning yourself to read and understand traditional legal writing. That's why no matter how hard you work, your first drafts will probably not be good plain-English documents. You can improve them by seeking feedback from your readers.

Prefer concrete, direct, everyday words; abandon legalisms, archaisms, and Latinisms; speak to the reader (Chapter 8)

Pay attention to your words. Develop a sense of which words nonlawyers are familiar with—then use them. Likewise, develop a sense of which words are lawyer-speak, unnecessary terms of art, and unnecessarily formal—then avoid them.

Construct simple sentences with a 20-word average (Chapter 9)

Once you've sensitized yourself to vocabulary, take control of your sentences. Identify and avoid the traditional legal-writing habits that plague most legal sentences.

Learn to use readability scales wisely (Chapter 10)

Your word processor can become a tool to aid you in producing plain English. But you'll need to understand what readability scales do, how they do it, and what they can't do. Once you know their strengths and limits, you can use them effectively.

8 Plain Legal Writing: Do It

The best sources on plain English

In writing this book, I've relied on the wisdom and expertise of many lawyers and writing experts. Today you can find numerous excellent sources on plain-English writing in the law. Here, I offer my choices for the best books on plain English.

A Plain Language Handbook for Legal Writers by Christine Mowat

This book takes a document-by-document approach to plain English and offers specific recommendations for each document. My favorite chapter is the one about wills, in which the author explains how she pushed her lawyer to prepare a plain-English will.

How to Write Plain English: A Book for Lawyers and Consumers by Rudolf Flesch

After he worked as a consultant for the Federal Communications Commission, Rudolf Flesch, the creator of the Flesch Reading Ease scale, wrote a book about his work. His tone is enthusiastic and motivational, and his advice is practical.

Lifting the Fog of Legalese by Joseph Kimble
Writing for Dollars, Writing to Please by Joseph Kimble

Professor Kimble is the leading expert on plain-English legal writing in the United States today. These books collect his articles and columns on the subject. Kimble's tone is forceful and persuasive, and he backs up what he says with research. In *Writing for Dollars*, he reports on dozens of studies proving the benefits, and savings, of plain-English legal writing.

Plain Language for Lawyers by Michèle M. Asprey

Asprey works in Australia and is one of the leading plain-English proponents in that country. Her book has lots of examples of outrageously bad legal writing. She also has an excellent chapter on testing plain English.

Plain and Accurate Style in Court Papers **by Irwin Alterman**

Although this book is now more than 25 years old, it is in many ways still ahead of its time. Alterman tracked the Federal Rules of Civil Procedure and offered excellent recommendations for bringing plainness to court documents. The book's principles are still relevant today.

Securities Disclosure in Plain English **by Bryan A. Garner**

Garner is the foremost expert on American English usage. In this book he explains how to conform to the Securities and Exchange Commission's (SEC) rules for plain English in prospectuses. The book is thorough and powerful. It also contains an example of a before-and-after prospectus as well as a copy of the SEC's own Plain English Handbook.

Writing Contracts in Plain English **by Carl Felsenfeld and Alan Siegel**

This is one of the earliest books to focus on improving legal documents intended for nonlegal readers. The authors are a lawyer and a language expert. Much of the book focuses on three consumer documents: a consumer-loan note, an apartment-sale contract, and a personal-liability insurance policy. This book encourages lawyers to write appropriately for the nonlegal audience. As the authors say: "The aim of plain English is to make functional documents function."[2]

Getting past the myths about plain legal language

Arm yourself. When someone tells you plain English won't work, rebut, respond, and press on.

By now you understand the basic principles of the plain-English movement: that legal writing intended for nonlawyers ought to be clear and readable to nonlawyers. But if you try to use it,

---

2. Carl Felsenfeld & Alan Siegel, *Writing Contracts in Plain English* 232 (1981).

10 Plain Legal Writing: Do It

you're bound to encounter resistance. Some resistance will come from others, but some of it will come from inside you. You're a lawyer, after all, and you have subconsciously accepted some myths about "plain" legal writing. I aim to debunk them.

Here are some myths about plain English

1. Plain English requires brevity, which isn't possible in many legal documents.
2. Plain English requires a literary style that isn't appropriate for legal writing.
3. Plain English lacks the precision of traditional legal language.
4. Plain English doesn't meet the expectations of clients.

Debunking the myths

1. The truth: plain English doesn't require brevity, but it often produces it.

This image of plain English—that it is only about shorter words and shorter sentences—is the most common misunderstanding of plain English. In the article "Against Plain English," a law professor named David Crump captured the essence of this myth when he asserted that "there is the model in which plain English refers to the brevity of the expression."[3]

Not so. Brevity isn't really the goal; it's a benefit. Besides, plain English has many attributes besides brevity. Make no mistake: brevity is highly valuable, as David Lambuth said in *The Golden Book on Writing*: "The fewer the words that can be made to convey an idea, the clearer and the more forceful that idea."[4]

But we plain-English types don't say shorter is always better, and we never say you must achieve brevity at the expense of clarity or accuracy. In fact, we say the opposite. In her book *Plain Language for Lawyers*, the Australian plain-English expert Michèle

---

3. David Crump, *Against Plain English: The Case for a Functional Approach to Legal Document Preparation*, 33 Rutgers L.J. 713, 728 (2002).
4. David Lambuth, *The Golden Book on Writing* 20 (1983).

Asprey says, "Brevity is one of the aims of plain language, but it is not the only one."[5] And as Peter Butt explains in *Modern Legal Drafting*, plain English accepts technical terms and "big" words if they're necessary: "While it shuns the antiquated and inflated word and phrase, which can readily be either omitted altogether or replaced with a more useful substitute, it does not seek to rid documents of terms which express important distinctions."[6]

Still, some lawyers believe this myth—that plain English would mean cutting all big words—and they offer these excuses:

- Excuse: Many big words are necessary terms of art.

But true terms of art are only a tiny part of all legal writing, and the existence of a few terms of art is no justification for the vast majority of bad legal writing that requires no terms of art. Experts on legal writing and legal drafting have been saying this for years. In *Legal Drafting in a Nutshell*, Thomas Haggard and George Kuney say that "specific words or phrases that absolutely must be used to achieve a particular result are relatively rare."[7] And in *Legal Writing: Sense and Nonsense*, David Mellinkoff says that "[w]here lawyers mislead themselves, and everyone else, is in believing that most of the words they use are terms of art."[8] Besides, plain English doesn't require us to drop all terms of art. It requires us instead to be sure that the word or phrase we're using actually is a term of art and that it is genuinely more precise than ordinary English.

- Excuse: Explaining law in plain English takes more words, not fewer.

This is true, and far from being a criticism of plain English, it's one of its tenets. Plain-English advocates teach that unnecessary

---

5. Asprey, supra note 1, at 306.
6. Peter Butt, *Modern Legal Drafting: A Guide to Using Clearer Language* 101 (3d ed. 2013).
7. Thomas R. Haggard & George W. Kuney, *Legal Drafting in a Nutshell* 190 (3d ed. 2007).
8. David Mellinkoff, *Legal Writing: Sense and Nonsense* 7 (1982).

words ought to be cut and that a long word should be replaced when there is a shorter equivalent. But plain-English advocates reject pompous legalisms even if the everyday-English substitute is longer or requires more words.

- Excuse: Legal language is specialized, so using ordinary words won't work.

Professor James White raised this concern in his 1985 book, *Heracles' Bow*, when he said that the plain-English movement would never go far because when you replace a legal word with an ordinary-English word, the law will eventually convert the ordinary word into a legal word.[9] But the plain-English movement is about a lot more than words. In fact, plain-English advocates are so universally acquainted with this uninformed "simple words" criticism that many try to preempt it by addressing it in their writing. Butt, for example, takes plain English well beyond words: "[P]lain language is concerned with matters of sentence and paragraph structure, with organization and design, where so many of the hindrances to clear expression originate."[10]

Similarly, Kimble explains in *Writing for Dollars, Writing to Please* that plain language isn't only about vocabulary. It involves all the techniques for clear communication—planning the document, designing it, organizing it, writing clear sentences, using plain words, and testing the document whenever possible on typical readers.[11]

Thus, anyone who reads the literature on plain English learns that plain English is about more than simple words. Reread the plain-English principles at the beginning of this chapter. Notice that word length and sentence length are important but that they're not the only things mentioned. This statement from Michèle Asprey ought to clear things up for good:

---

9. James Boyd White, *Heracles' Bow: Essays on the Rhetoric and Poetics of the Law* 71–72 (1985).
10. Butt, *supra* note 5, at 101.
11. Joseph Kimble, *Writing for Dollars, Writing to Please* 21–22 (2012).

Plain-language drafting is more than just a matter of using simple words. Less than half this book is devoted to words. The rest looks at writing for your audience, choosing the appropriate tone, planning, structure, design and layout, readability, devices to help your reader find things, testing, and some "philosophical" matters.[12]

2. The truth: plain English doesn't require literary style.

The myth holds that plain-English advocates want lawyers to write like Ernest Hemingway, or at least like a succinct novelist. Richard Hyland seems to be the one who set up this myth in his 1986 article "A Defense of Legal Writing." He said that critics of traditional legal writing—the plain-English crowd—have "an idea implicit in their suggestions for improvement: namely that lawyers should write like novelists."[13] It's obvious why he had to say the idea was implicit. In reality, plain-English advocates don't say that at all.

In my experience, the only people who portray "literary style" as a goal of the plain-English movement are those who are criticizing plain English. That's what Professor Crump did in "Against Plain English," in which he said that "rewriting a tested, proven formula into a more literary style, of one's own invention, is inadvisable."[14] But plain-English advocates don't suggest that lawyers rewrite their forms in a literary style. This argument is a straw figure that's too easy to knock down.

Granted, some experts say plain English can be enjoyable to read. But no legal-writing expert asserts that a loan agreement ought to be written like a Hemingway novel. Plain-English advocates temper the aspiration to write clearly and plainly with the realities of legal practice. For example, here is what Ronald Goldfarb and James Raymond say in their book *Clear Understandings* about lawyers trying to write plainly:

---

12. Asprey, *supra* note 1, at 197.
13. Richard Hyland, *A Defense of Legal Writing*, 134 U. Pa. L. Rev. 599, 599 (1986).
14. Crump, *supra* note 2, at 725.

> We are not so naïve as to suppose that lawyers should write like journalists or novelists, or that their prose should always be entertaining as well as instructive. On the other hand, we are persuaded that lawyers who have distinguished themselves as great writers have in common with other good writers certain techniques, certain resources, certain sensibilities to the nuances of language that enrich the law, not encumber it, making its expression both pleasurable and precise.[15]

As with the brevity myth, this misplaced criticism is common enough that experts have addressed it. In *Modern Legal Drafting*, Butt admits that "a legal document will never read like a good novel, but it can be attractive and effective in a clean, clear, functional style."[16]

To say that plain-English advocates insist that legal writing be "literary" is to misunderstand the aims of the plain-English movement and to be ignorant of the literature on plain English. Legal-writing expert Mark Mathewson reiterates that point in a piece he wrote responding to Hyland. That piece is called "A Critic of Plain English Misses the Mark," and in it Mathewson says this: "Lawyers should write like novelists? If that were truly what plain-language advocates thought, Hyland could rightly dismiss them, but that's not what they think, at least none that I've read."[17]

3. The truth: plain English doesn't lack precision.

This raises two related excuses for not writing in plain English: that traditional legal language is more precise than plain English and that traditional legal language is based on reliable precedent.

The precision excuse. This excuse is usually mentioned by lawyers and law professors as a stock response whenever someone calls for plain English. But it also shows up in print. Professor

---

15. Ronald L. Goldfarb & James C. Raymond, *Clear Understandings: A Guide to Legal Writing* xv (1982).
16. Butt, *supra* note 5, at 95.
17. Mark Mathewson, *A Critic of Plain English Misses the Mark*, 8 Scribes J. Legal Writing 147, 148 (2001–2002).

Crump perpetuated this excuse in "Against Plain English." He asserted that traditional phrases are more precise than plain-English phrases.[18]

Anyone who challenges plain English on precision ought to carry out the following exercise. Pick a traditional legal word or phrase. Look it up in a legal-usage dictionary and in *Words and Phrases* (the West publication that collects judicially created definitions). Then figure out if the traditional legal word is really more precise than the ordinary word. Usually, it's not.

Those who challenge plain-English advocates on precision need to read Joseph Kimble's *Lifting the Fog of Legalese*, especially the chapter on "The Great Myth That Plain Language Is Not Precise." He says the choice is not between plain English and precision, because there cannot be perfect precision in written English. So the choice is really between imprecise writing in plain English and imprecise writing in the dense fog of legalese.[19] Kimble prefers plain English, as do I.

More important, as Kimble asserts in *Writing for Dollars*, plain English and precision are complementary. Plain language is more precise than traditional legal writing because it uncovers the ambiguities and errors that traditional style, with all its excesses, tends to hide.[20] And Kimble presents, in both *Lifting the Fog* and *Writing for Dollars*, dozens of real-world examples of companies, government agencies, and individuals improving documents and saving money by using plain English.

Other experts agree. Butt says—

> [P]lain English is as capable of precision as traditional legal English. It can cope with all the concepts and complexities of the law and legal processes. The few technical terms that the lawyer might feel

---

18. Crump, *supra* note 2, at 732.
19. Joseph Kimble, *Lifting the Fog of Legalese* 45 (2006).
20. Kimble, *supra* note 10, at 37.

compelled to retain for convenience or necessity can be incorporated without destroying the document's integrity.[21]

The precedent excuse. The excuse of precision itself relies on another great excuse in legal writing. Those who say that traditional legal language is more precise than ordinary English rely on this venerated but questionable proposition: Once legal language has been construed by a court, its meaning is clear; it ought to be set in stone.

Isn't it just as likely that the next judge, confronted with the same language in a different factual context, will say it means something else? It's not too hard to figure out. Look through *Words and Phrases*. A few minutes in there ought to dispel the idea that judges are consistent in assigning meaning to legal language. Mellinkoff calls *Words and Phrases* "an impressive demonstration of lack of precision in the language of the law."[22]

Yet the precedent excuse—that courts construe legal words and give them reliable meanings—often goes unchallenged. Mellinkoff challenged the idea in *The Language of the Law* in 1963. And he convincingly debunked the idea that litigation-tested language makes good form book material.[23]

In my view, Michèle Asprey got it right: "So how comfortable should we feel when we say that a word has years of case law behind it which tells us what it meant? Surely what we are actually saying is that people have been arguing over its meaning in various contexts for years."[24]

4. The truth: clients don't prefer legalese.

Writing in a traditional, dense, and archaic legal style is sometimes treated as a full-employment plan for lawyers. If clients could

---

21. Butt, *supra* note 5, at 95.
22. David Mellinkoff, *The Language of the Law* 375 (1963).
23. *Id.* at 278–82.
24. Asprey, *supra* note 1, at 24.

understand what we write, some say, they wouldn't need the lawyers. This thinking relies on some questionable premises.

- Excuse: Clients take legalese seriously because it's impressive.

Clients do take some legalese seriously. The legal linguist Peter Tiersma suggests in his book *Legal Language* that "in the courtroom, verbal formulas and ritualistic words put the audience on notice that this is a proceeding with important consequences."[25] But he goes on to question the value of this formal language more generally: "Even though formal legal language may serve some purpose, we should ponder whether that goal might not be carried out just as well by some other means, one that does less injury to the goal of clear communication."[26]

After all, it is the legal effect of words, not their emotional impact, that is important in most legal writing. Of course, jury arguments and persuasive briefs are a different matter. But if a drafted document says what it legally needs to say, even in simple terms, a court should enforce it. Besides, are clients really impressed with traditional legal language? Generally, no. Here's what two nonlawyer writing experts have to say about lawyers' justifications for traditional legal writing:

> [W]e outsiders are not persuaded. We suspect that lawyers use the old language at times because it is conveniently available in form books, or because it makes them sound like lawyers, or because they are blissfully unaware of how odd it really is, or because they think it will fill us outsiders with awe and a willingness to pay handsomely for documents beyond our ken. We even suspect that on occasion lawyers themselves do not understand the language of the law.[27]

---

25. Peter M. Tiersma, *Legal Language* 102–03 (1999).
26. *Id.*
27. Louise Mailhot & James D. Carnwath, *Decisions, Decisions ... A Handbook for Judicial Writing* XIV (1998).

- Excuse: Clients expect and prefer traditional legal language.

I haven't met a client who has said this. Only lawyers say this, on behalf of clients. Is it true? I doubt it.

In one study conducted in Australia, nonlawyer clients reported that understanding what a lawyer had written for them was important: "These people said they wanted their lawyers to give them practical, commercial advice which they could actually use to solve their problems—and they wanted it in plain language."[28] These clients, at least, seemed to prefer plain English to traditional legal language.

Plain-English advocates and drafting experts today remind lawyers again and again that we must try to draft documents—as much as possible—so nonlawyer clients can understand them. Michèle Asprey writes that "We cannot continue to pretend that legal writing is meant to be read and used only by lawyers."[29] And Howard Darmstadter suggests a new model for preparing legal documents: "A legal document should teach a reader how a transaction works."[30]

Today, more and more clients want to know what their lawyers are doing for them, and they're willing to find a new lawyer who can explain things clearly. More and more clients have gotten the notion that if you're a professional, you should be able to explain complex matters in plain English.

Still, some lawyers believe they'll put themselves out of business if they don't write complicated documents. They believe, according to Robert Dick in his book *Legal Drafting in Plain Language*, that a "client comes to the office to receive a lengthy magic document of the deepest obscurity." But Dick questioned this theory: "Why obscurity should promote a lawyer's practice is difficult to understand .... Modern clients reject this approach and are no

---

28. Asprey, *supra* note 1, at 68–69.
29. *Id.* at 8.
30. Howard Darmstadter, *Hereof, Thereof, and Everywhereof: A Contrarian Guide to Legal Drafting* 25 (2002).

longer impressed with the hocus-pocus."[31] In fact, many clients deride the traditional approach. Carl Felsenfeld and Alan Siegel, in *Writing Contracts in Plain English*, recognized that "ponderous language may create an illusion of precision. Among lay readers, it invites ridicule."[32]

And finally, more and more lawyers are realizing that traditional, convoluted legal drafting doesn't retain clients—it pushes them away. According to Butt: "Few things have done more to drive people from our doors than our inability both in documents and in letters and speech to express ourselves in clear simple English."[33]

Plain-English advocates aren't blind zealots. We acknowledge the value of terms of art, of form books, and of certain solemn legal language. We understand that all those things have their places, but we insist that those places are small. Those limited uses should not be allowed to override the need to change legal writing in almost every other area.

Plain-English advocates also believe that clear and plain legal writing brings respect, appreciation, and clients.

---

31. *Id.*
32. Carl Felsenfeld & Alan Siegel, *Writing Contracts in Plain English* 144 (1981).
33. Butt, *supra* note 5, at 91.

A Plain-English Drafting Process

Question, and master, your forms. Then implement a systematic process for creating a plain-English document.

The realities of forms

Nearly all plain legal drafting results from converting an existing form into plain English. Of course, there are times when you'll be drafting from scratch. If so, apply the principles in this book to produce plain legal drafting. But if, as is usually the case, you're using a form, keep in mind some key advice.

First, although you may be able to rely on a form for substantive content, you should almost never rely on it for expressing that content. Most forms are, by their very nature, outdated. Many, in fact, contain dreadful legalese, archaic word usage, and other drafting errors. Question everything about a form—especially the language.

Second, apply your drafting skills to a form as carefully as you would when drafting from scratch. Forms tend to induce haste, laziness, and complacency. Be sure you know all the content, and be sure you revise the form appropriately for your current transaction. In other words, master the form. For more on the challenges of using forms, see Chapter 4.

Third, have the guts to cut down the length and size of the form. Nearly all form documents grow by accretion. They almost never shrink. Typically, the drafter will think that any provision

22 Plain Legal Writing: Do It

that was useful on the last transaction can't hurt this transaction, and so the accreted provisions multiply. For plain legal drafting, you must cut the provisions that aren't necessary or that don't relate to your transaction.

With these attitudes and approaches in mind, you're ready to prepare a plain-English document by revising a traditional form.

A process for plain-English revising

Once you have a reliable form to use for your transaction, how should you go about revising it into plain English? I recommend a five-step process.

Step 1: Read the entire document from beginning to end. You're trying to get a sense of the content and complexity of the text. This is hard for most lawyers, because even though it's helpful to read straight through without stopping, lawyers have an editor's mentality. We want to markup changes to the document. Okay, a little marking won't hurt now. In fact, I often find myself highlighting words and phrases and taking brief notes at this stage. But don't forget the purpose of this first reading: you need to get to know what the document is doing.

Step 2: Create a list of the substantive content. I do this by creating a separate document called "[name of document] content." My content document is nothing more than an exhaustive list of every substantive item in the original. I create this content document for two reasons: (1) to help me master the content, and (2) to use as a checklist when I produce a revision. I use the checklist to be sure my revision contains the same content as the original. (Remember the underlying premise of this book: it's about the language, not the substance. In my plain-English work, I keep the substance the same to the greatest extent I can.)

Step 3: Sort and order the content list. Think about the needs of the reader, the most important topics in the document, the order in which the transaction will be carried out, and other considerations. Group related concepts together, and begin thinking about headings, subheadings, and numbering. Feel free to question and change the order of the original. Consider placing a summary first.

Step 4: Rewrite the text in plain English, applying the principles in this book. In this step, I often work directly from my sorted content list, keeping the original document handy as a reference. This approach helps free you from the original language, which is probably poor, but keeps you closely tied to the necessary content.

Step 5: Revise and edit your new document. Naturally, the basic principles of editing apply here. Try to give yourself some time away from the document before you edit; this distance will allow you to bring a fresh perspective to the text. Devote a substantial amount of time to the edit; experts recommend as much as 50 percent of the total time on the project. Ask others to read and comment on the text; include one lawyer who is an expert on the subject and one nonlawyer who is unfamiliar with the subject. (You may decide to test the document on its intended audience. See Chapter 7 on testing.)

An example of the process

The following text is excerpted from a real class-action notice. The names have been changed. Given that this notice was sent to ordinary consumers, most of whom have no legal training, I think the original text is particularly poor. It's complicated, legalistic, poorly designed, and uninviting.

We can take this text through the five-step process for converting to plain English.

Step 1: Read the entire text from beginning to end.

Pardon my commentary in the bullets—I couldn't help myself.

Original class-action notice

> TO: ALL RECORD AND BENEFICIAL HOLDERS OF THE COMMON STOCK OF ETRA, INC. (THE "COMPANY"), INCLUDING ALL OF ITS PREDECESSORS, DURING THE PERIOD BEGINNING ON AND INCLUDING JANUARY 1, 1995 THROUGH AND INCLUDING MARCH 22, 2007.

24 Plain Legal Writing: Do It

- Is a nonlawyer going to understand what record holders are? Beneficial holders? Also, the all-caps text makes it hard to read.

PLEASE READ THIS NOTICE CAREFULLY AND IN ITS ENTIRETY. YOUR RIGHTS MAY BE AFFECTED BY THE LEGAL PROCEEDINGS IN THIS LITIGATION. BROKERAGE FIRMS, BANKS, AND OTHER PERSONS OR ENTITIES WHO ARE MEMBERS OF THE CLASS IN THEIR CAPACITIES AS RECORD OWNERS, BUT NOT AS BENEFICIAL OWNERS, ARE DIRECTED TO SEND THIS NOTICE PROMPTLY TO BENEFICIAL OWNERS.

- This paragraph mixes an instruction to read the document carefully with an instruction to brokers and other agents who, given the subject matter, are certainly more sophisticated than the typical readers. That's confusing. Notice that it's switched from "holders" to "owners." Why? And also notice there's more all-caps text.

The purpose of the notice is to inform you of this lawsuit (the "Action"), a proposed settlement of the Action (the "Settlement"), and a hearing to be held by the Circuit Court (the "Court"), on October 5, 2007, at 1 p.m. (the "Settlement Hearing"), at which the Court shall consider for approval: (i) whether this Action will be certified as a class action, for settlement purposes only, pursuant to Rule of Civil Procedure 23; (ii) whether the terms and conditions of the Settlement are fair, reasonable, adequate, and in the best interests of the Class and the Company; (iii) whether the Final Order should be entered dismissing this Action with prejudice as against Plaintiffs and the Class, releasing the Settled Claims, and enjoining prosecution of any and all Settled Claims; (iv) the award of Plaintiffs' counsel's attorneys' fees and expenses as provided for herein, as to which award Company has agreed to pay $7.5 million; (v) any objections to the Settlement; and (vi) such other relief as the Court may deem necessary and appropriate. Any of the dates set forth herein may be modified by the Court without further notice. The Court reserves the right to approve the Settlement at or after the Settlement Hearing with such modifications as may be consented to by the parties to the Stipulation and without further notice to the Class.

This long, dense paragraph is difficult to read and understand. By creating and defining a series of shorthand terms, it foists excessive clutter on readers. In fact, it also uses some terms that haven't been defined: Final Order, Plaintiffs, and Stipulation. It's unnecessarily formal in tone and uses legalistic romanettes for numbering. Let's continue:

> THE DESCRIPTION OF THE ACTION AND THE SETTLEMENT WHICH FOLLOWS HAS BEEN PREPARED BY COUNSEL FOR THE PARTIES. THE COURT HAS MADE NO FINDING WITH RESPECT TO SUCH MATTERS, AND THIS NOTICE IS NOT AN EXPRESSION OR STATEMENT BY THE COURT OF FINDINGS OF FACT.

- The text is highly legalistic in tone and uses some insider jargon: such, findings of fact. Again, the use of all-caps text is unnecessary.

Step 2: Create a list of the document's substantive content.

Here's my list of the substantive content divided into single-sentence concepts.

- Address the record and beneficial owners of Etra and its predecessors' stock from January 1, 1995, to March 22, 2007.
- Instruction to read the notice carefully and fully. The hearing described here may affect your rights.
- Instructions to brokers and agents who hold Etra stock as record owners to forward this notice to beneficial owners.
- Inform you of this lawsuit, a proposed settlement, and a hearing.
- Details of the hearing: held by the Circuit Court on October 5, 2007, at 1 p.m. Items the court will consider:
- whether to certify a class action for settlement under Fed. R. Civ. P. 23;

- whether the terms of the settlement are fair, reasonable, adequate, and in the best interests of the class and the company;
- whether to dismiss this case with prejudice, release the settled claims, and enjoin pursuit of settled claims;
- whether to award Plaintiffs' lawyers fees and expenses of $7.5 million as agreed by the company;
- objections to the settlement;
- other relief the court decides is necessary and appropriate.
- Inform you that the court may change the dates without notice.
- Inform you that the court can approve the settlement at or after the hearing and may make changes with the parties' consent without notice to the class.
- Inform you that the lawyers prepared this document, not the court.
- Inform you that the court has not made any findings of fact.

Step 3: Sort and order the content list.

The order of the original was good. I agree that we should begin with by addressing those receiving the notice, and an instruction to read it carefully seems important to have up front, too. Plus, an instruction to brokers and agents to inform beneficial owners should be near the top as well. I'll leave those parts intact.

Here's the first part of my sorted and ordered list:

1. Address the record and beneficial owners of Etra—and predecessors'—stock from January 1, 1995, to March 22, 2007.
2. Instruction to read the notice carefully and fully. The hearing described here may affect your rights.
3. Instructions to brokers and agents who hold Etra stock as record owners to forward this notice to beneficial owners.

It's also hard to quibble with the order of the next section: stating the purpose of the document, the date of the hearing, and then

Plain-English Drafting Process 27

the details of the hearing—this seems a logical order. But I might adjust the order of the items just a bit. Possible dismissal ought to come first, and objections to the settlement ought to come after consideration of the other aspects of the settlement.

4. Inform you of this lawsuit, a proposed settlement, and a hearing.

5. Details of the hearing: held by the Circuit Court on October 5, 2007, at 1 p.m. Items the court will consider:

    - whether to dismiss this case with prejudice, release the settled claims, and enjoin pursuit of settled claims;
    - whether to certify a class action for settlement under Rule 23;
    - whether the terms of the settlement are fair, reasonable, adequate, and in the best interests of the class and the company;
    - objections to the settlement;
    - whether to award Plaintiffs' lawyers fees and expenses of $7.5 million as agreed by the company;
    - other relief as the court decides is necessary and appropriate.

6. Inform you that the court may change the dates without notice.

7. Inform you that the court can approve the settlement at or after the hearing and may make changes with the parties' consent without notice to the class.

8. Inform you that the lawyers prepared this document, not the court.

    9. Inform you that the court has not made any findings of fact.

Step 4: Rewrite the document in plain English.

Now I'll rewrite the text in plain English without making substantive changes. If you think I've failed to get the substance right or changed the content in some way, I can live with that. I'll need to consult an expert on class actions as part of Step 5 anyway. What's more, please remember that critiques of content are critiques of my knowledge of class-action law, not of plain English.

First revised class-action notice

If you owned common stock in Etra, Inc. between January 1, 1995, and March 22, 2007, you may have rights in a class-action lawsuit.

> Read this notice carefully—it affects your rights.
>
> Brokers and agents: forward this notice to beneficial owners of Etra common stock.
>
> This class-action lawsuit may be settled. This notice explains the details and how you can participate if you want to.
>
> The judge will hold a hearing about the settlement on October 5, 2007. At the hearing, the judge will consider these things:
> - whether to dismiss this lawsuit and prevent the plaintiffs from suing again;
> - whether to approve this lawsuit as a class action;
> - whether the settlement is fair, reasonable, adequate, and in the best interests of the class and Etra;
> - whether there are any objections to the settlement;
> - whether to give the plaintiffs' lawyers $7.5 million in fees and expenses—which Etra has agreed to pay;
> - anything else the judge thinks is appropriate.
>
> The judge can change the dates without notice, and the judge can approve the settlement at the hearing or later. If the parties agree, the judge can change the details of the settlement without notice to the class.
>
> The lawyers prepared this document, not the judge. The judge has not made any decisions yet.

Step 5: Revise and edit the document.

For this final edit, I'll reformat the text for emphasis and to highlight key information. The final form of this revision also implements techniques recommended by the Federal Judicial Center in its sample class-action notices.[1]

Final revised class-action notice

If you owned stock in Etra, Inc. between January 1, 1995, and March 22, 2007, you may have rights in a class-action lawsuit.

Read this notice carefully—it affects your rights.

Brokers and agents: forward this notice to beneficial owners of Etra stock.

This class-action lawsuit may be settled. This notice explains the details and how you can participate in the settlement if you want to.

The judge will hold a hearing about the settlement on October 5, 2007. At the hearing, the judge will consider these things:

- whether to dismiss this lawsuit and prevent the plaintiffs from suing again;
- whether to approve this lawsuit as a class action;
- whether the settlement is fair, reasonable, adequate, and in the best interests of the class and Etra;
- whether there are any objections to the settlement;
- whether to give the plaintiffs' lawyers $7.5 million in fees and expenses—which Etra has agreed to pay;
- anything else the judge thinks is appropriate.

The judge can change the date without notice, and the judge can approve the settlement at the hearing or later. If the parties agree, the judge can change the details of the settlement without notice to the class.

The lawyers prepared this document, not the judge.

---

1. https://www.fjc.gov/content/301253/illustrative-forms-class-action-notices-introduction

> The judge has not made any decisions yet.

The before-and-after versions of this class-action notice are also in the before-and-after chapter at the end of the book.

That's the process. Now that we have a process in place, we can begin studying the specific techniques that will help us make documents readable and plain.

Designing Plain Legal Documents

In plain-English documents, use modern typographic principles and format the text for easy reading and easy skimming. Abandon the relics of the typewriter.

The way your document looks can invite readers into the document or put them off. The way your document is presented will either allow them to read it quickly and easily or make their eyes and minds tired. And the way your document is designed will either ease skimming (the way we all read) or make skimming difficult. This chapter acknowledges the way readers read and presents some basic principles of modern, professional document design. For a comprehensive guide to legal-document layout and format, see Matthew Butterick, *Typography for Lawyers* (2d ed. 2018).

Fonts

The two most important types of fonts you will use in documents for nonlawyers are serifed fonts and sans-serif fonts.

Serifed fonts have serifs, or small extensions, at the ends of the strokes. These serifs make each letter distinct and allow the eye to seize upon these distinctions more quickly, thus easing the reader's way. Common serifed fonts are

- Times New Roman
- Cambria
- Georgia

Because serifed fonts are generally regarded as the easiest to read when printed on paper, the main body of your text should probably be in a serifed font. Take a look at the books, newspapers, and magazines you read each day. The main text in most of these publications is in a serifed font.

The next type of font you'll use in documents for nonlawyers is sans serif. Sans-serif fonts do not have serifs at the end of each stroke, and they generally look more modern and informal than serifed fonts. Some common sans-serif fonts are

- Arial
- Calibri
- Tahoma

Sans-serif fonts are generally considered easier to read on a computer screen than serifed fonts because screen resolutions make the serifs harder to see. If you know your legal document will be read primarily on the screen, you might want to use a sans-serif font.

Is it okay to use more than one font in a single document? Yes it is, and one good recommendation is to use a serifed font for the main text and a sans serif, boldface font for short topic headings. This creates a strong contrast between the headings and the main text, making the headings stand out and allowing the reader to skim the headings more easily. That's the practice used in this book.

A final note: The one mistake that no modern legal writer should make today is to use a Courier font. Courier is a relic of the typewriter. It uses a lot of space on the page and looks old-fashioned.

Type styles

Many legal documents use ALL-CAPITALS TEXT and underlining. For readable and skimmable documents, you should abandon all caps and underlining. These two type styles were used when lawyers prepared their documents on typewriters. Typewriters couldn't create boldface (although I guess you could pound the keys really hard) or italics, so we used all capitals in place of boldface and underlining in place of italics. We did this to mimic the type styles used in professionally printed documents.

Today, word processors allow us to accurately mimic the type styles of professionally printed documents. Modern legal documents should avoid the relics of the typewriter. Use boldface and italics in place of all capitals and underlining.

Besides being difficult to read because of the uniform height of the characters, all-capitals text is off-putting, AND CAN COME ACROSS AS SHOUTING at the reader. Underlined text is also more difficult to read than regular type, at least partly because the underline obscures the descending portion of the letters g, j, p, q, and y, like this: gjpqy.

For more information on the vestiges of the typewriter in modern documents and what you can do about them in your own documents, see the following resources:

- Robin Williams, *The PC Is Not a Typewriter* (1995)
- Robin Williams, *The Mac Is Not a Typewriter* (2d ed. 2003)
- Ruth Anne Robbins, *Painting with Print: Incorporating Concepts of Typographic and Layout Design into the Text of Legal Writing Documents*, 2 J. ALWD 108 (2004)
- Derek H. Keirnan-Johnson, *Telling through Type: Typography and Narrative in Legal Briefs*, 7 J. ALWD 88 (2010)

Creating emphasis

A good way to create emphasis in documents for nonlawyers is to use boldface type. In many legal documents, especially those aimed at nonlawyers, certain parts of the text must be emphasized, or presented in a way that is conspicuous. In many of these documents, lawyers try to achieve conspicuousness and emphasis by using all-capitals text. Although all-caps text certainly draws the reader's attention because it stands out from the rest of the text, once the reader tries to read the text, it'll be slow going. Better to put the conspicuous text in boldface type.

So if the original text looks like this:

34 Plain Legal Writing: Do It

> THE HOLDER ASSUMES ALL RISK AND DANGERS INCIDENTAL TO THE GAME OF BASEBALL INCLUDING SPECIFICALLY (BUT NOT EXCLUSIVELY) THE DANGER OF BEING INJURED BY THROWN OR BATTED BALLS AND AGREES THAT THE PARTICIPATING CLUBS, THEIR AGENTS AND PLAYERS ARE NOT LIABLE FOR INJURIES RESULTING FROM SUCH CAUSES.

then you should use boldface instead:

> **The holder assumes all risk and dangers incidental to the game of baseball including specifically (but not exclusively) the danger of being injured by thrown or batted balls and agrees that the participating clubs, their agents and players are not liable for injuries resulting from such causes.**

If other provisions in the document are in boldface type, or if the headings in the document are in boldface type, boldface alone might not satisfy someone who is persnickety about emphasis—a court, for example. So if you want to create conspicuous text, you can use more than one technique. Here's an example of three techniques applied to create emphasis and conspicuousness: boldface type, smaller type size, and a box. It looks like this:

> The holder assumes all risk and dangers incidental to the game of baseball including specifically (but not exclusively) the danger of being injured by thrown or batted balls and agrees that the participating clubs, their agents and players are not liable for injuries resulting from such causes.

Some might raise a concern that if the goal is to make text conspicuous, you shouldn't make it smaller than the surrounding text, as that minimizes it. But what's important for conspicuousness is not size per se but contrast. To enhance the contrast, the approach above uses three design elements: (1) the box draws attention to the text and sets it off, (2) the boldface type makes the text stand out from the surrounding text, and (3) the smaller type size contrasts the text with the surrounding text.

Finally, don't use initial capitals to create emphasis in text, like this:

The Holder Is Admitted on Condition, and by Use of this Ticket Agrees, That He Will Not Transmit or Aid in Transmitting Any Description, Account, Picture or Reproduction of the Baseball Game or Exhibition to Which this Ticket Admits Him. Breach of the Foregoing Will Automatically Terminate this License.

Reserve initial capitals for titles, proper nouns, and defined terms.

Line length

If the document is to be readable and skimmable, a line of text across the page shouldn't be too long. Line length is measured in characters and includes spaces. For example:

This line has 28 characters.

Generally speaking, experts recommend line lengths of 50 to 80 characters. The longer the line length, the harder it is for the reader's eyes to move back to the left margin after finishing a line. But word processors generally don't have a way to set the line length. You manage line length with type size and margins. For example, these two lines have the same number of characters and are both in 10-point type, but because they use different fonts, they take up different amounts of space:

This line has 28 characters.
This line has 28 characters.

The default settings on Microsoft Word these days—1-inch margins left and right and Calibri, 11-point type—will create line lengths that are too long. To improve the readability of your documents, you can move your margins in to 1.25 inches on the left and right, and you can choose another font (I like Cambria) and increase the type size to 12 points. But you have other options. You can use a font that takes up more space than Calibri, such as Century Schoolbook or Georgia. (Besides, Calibri isn't ideal for body text because it's a sans serif font.)

Suppose you need to get a lot of text onto a single page—maybe the client wants the entire document to fit on one page. Making the

36 Plain Legal Writing: Do It

text fit by shrinking the type will make it too hard to read, right? Not necessarily. As long as the type isn't tiny, the main concern is the line length, not type size. Look at a print newspaper. Newspapers use small type and get away with it. How? By shortening the line length and using columns. You can break a document into two columns and use a smaller type size because the line lengths will still be manageable.

For example, text in a small font, such as 9 points, with a long line length looks like this:

Disclaimer

The holder is admitted on condition, and by use of this ticket agrees, that he will not transmit or aid in transmitting any description, account, picture or reproduction of the baseball game or exhibition to which this ticket admits him. Breach of the foregoing will automatically terminate this license.

The holder assumes all risk and dangers incidental to the game of baseball including specifically (but not exclusively) the danger of being injured by thrown or batted balls and agrees that the participating clubs, their agents and players are not liable for injuries resulting from such causes. The management reserves the right to revoke the license granted by this ticket.

But this text can still be readable if you use columns, like this:

Disclaimer

The holder is admitted on condition, and by use of this ticket agrees, that he will not transmit or aid in transmitting any description, account, picture or reproduction of the baseball game or exhibition to which this ticket admits him. Breach of the foregoing will automatically terminate this license.

The holder assumes all risk and dangers incidental to the game of baseball including specifically (but not exclusively) the danger of being injured by thrown or batted balls and agrees that the participating clubs, their agents and players are not liable for injuries resulting from such causes. The management reserves the right to revoke the license granted by this ticket.

Note: I don't recommend columns for a document that will be read on a screen. It gives you a headache when you have to scroll up and down repeatedly.

By the way, if you look at a single-spaced document with 1-inch margins on the left and right and Calibri 11-point type (or Times New Roman 12-point type), it will surely look dense and crowded. As I've said, pushing the margins in to 1.25 inches on the left and right and increasing the type size will greatly improve the readability of the document, at least partly because it will shorten the line length. But lawyers sometimes do something else to eliminate the crowded look of the default settings: double-spacing.

I don't care for double spacing; it uses more paper, lengthens the document, and reduces the number of headings and paragraphs per page, which make text harder to skim. Besides, I'm able to read books, magazines, and newspapers quite easily, and none of them are double-spaced. So I don't recommend double-spacing for plain-English documents.

Justification: center, full, and left

Generally speaking, you shouldn't center the text in a typical legal document. It's simply too hard to read. In fact, sentence-length, explanatory headings should usually be noncentered. Placing them on the left margin will make the document easier to skim because all the headings line up. For me, only titles and topic headings should be centered.

The real question is whether you should left justify or fully justify your documents. Fully justified text tends to look neater on the page because there are clean vertical lines on the left and right margins. Most books, magazines, and newspapers are fully justified, and your word processor is capable of fully justifying your text.

The drawback of using full justification is that your word processor is not as sophisticated as the programs used for the professionally printed documents you usually read. If you fully justify your legal documents, you'll often see odd gaps and spaces in the text. Of course, you can improve the look of the justified text by using the hyphenation function, which breaks words at the right margin and inserts a hyphen. That's the practice used in this book.

38 Plain Legal Writing: Do It

But this can be tedious because you need to be sure that every broken word is correctly hyphenated between syllables.

Here's my advice: if the fully justified text looks neat and clean and doesn't have odd gaps or spaces, then full justification is appropriate. Otherwise, left justification, which leaves a ragged right margin, is entirely appropriate for legal documents.

Numbering

In plain-English transactional documents, a comprehensive numbering system can be useful for readers, especially if the document is long. The numbering provides a sense of priority and order and makes it easy to refer to any specific provision in the document. I recommend numbering for any long transactional document. In numbering your document, be sure to number every separate section, paragraph, and clause in the document. Don't leave unnumbered or "dangling" text.

Not every document needs a numbering system. Many short consumer-transaction documents are better without numbering, and court documents and letters generally don't need numbering. In these documents, numbering tends to make the document seem more formal and cluttered.

If you're going to use a numbering system, I offer three suggestions.

First, don't use roman numerals (I, V, X, and so on) or romanettes (i, v, x, and so on). These lend an air of formality to a plain-English document that isn't called for. And if your document has a lot of numbers, roman numerals will eventually become hard to decipher. Besides, we have a perfectly good system of numerals, called the Arabic system (1, 2, 3, and so on).

Second, use proper alignment. Avoid large tabs (I recommend 0.25 inches instead of 0.5) and overtabbing. Use indentation to create vertical alignment and keep the document neat and readable. For example, the following text has poor alignment, with large tabs, overtabbing, and no indentation:

    1.   **Disclaimer**

1.1 The holder is admitted on condition, and by use of this ticket agrees, that he will not transmit or aid in transmitting any description, account, picture or reproduction of the baseball game or exhibition to which this ticket admits him. Breach of the foregoing will automatically terminate this license.

This text is properly aligned, with shorter tabs, fewer tabs, and indentation. It looks better and is easier to read:

1. **Disclaimer**
1.1 The holder is admitted on condition, and by use of this ticket agrees, that he will not transmit or aid in transmitting any description, account, picture or reproduction of the baseball game or exhibition to which this ticket admits him. Breach of the foregoing will automatically terminate this license.

Third, use a sensible numbering system. I like this one:

1. (topic or article)
1.1 (section)
1.1(a) (subsection)
1.1(a)(1) (paragraph)

This numbering system gives you four levels for the document. If you need more than four levels, the document is probably too complex or you are over-subdividing it. For more on numbering your document, see Chapter 5.

Footers

In a multi-page document, it's helpful to include a running footer. The text of the footer could contain the document's title or description and a page number. The page-number display might also contain an "of page" designation: 3 of 6, 4 of 6, and so on. The footer might also contain a file name for internal use.

Endnotes and footnotes

Transactional documents rarely contain citations to authority and almost never contain endnotes or footnotes. If you're writing a court document or letter, try to avoid using endnotes and footnotes.

40 Plain Legal Writing: Do It

If you must, footnotes are better. Although footnotes force readers to nod their heads up and down, endnotes are worse because they force readers to flip back and forth between the text and the end of the document.

Tables

Using graphics in your text can ease the reader's way. One especially helpful technique is the if-then table. The if-then table makes it easier for the reader to understand choices and see the options. Here is a good example:

For book sales of	The royalty percentage is
1–499	10%
500–999	15%
1000 or more	20%

An example of document-design techniques

The following example contains many document-design weaknesses:

- use of Courier (an outdated typeface)
- use of all-capitals type for emphasis
- use of same font for heading
- use of underlining

Before

```
                    DISCLAIMER
    The holder is admitted on condition, and by
use of this ticket agrees, that he will not
transmit or aid in transmitting any descrip-
tion, account, picture or reproduction of the
baseball game or exhibition to which this
ticket admits him. Breach of the foregoing
will automatically terminate this license.
    THE HOLDER ASSUMES ALL RISK AND DANGERS IN-
CIDENTAL TO THE GAME OF BASEBALL INCLUDING
SPECIFICALLY (BUT NOT EXCLUSIVELY) THE DANGER
OF BEING INJURED BY THROWN OR BATTED BALLS AND
```

```
AGREES THAT THE PARTICIPATING CLUBS, THEIR
AGENTS AND PLAYERS ARE NOT LIABLE FOR INJURIES
RESULTING FROM SUCH CAUSES.
   The management reserves the right to revoke
the license granted by this ticket.
```

The revision below uses better document-design techniques:

- use of a contrasting typeface for the heading
- use of left-aligned headings
- use of a modern serifed font
- use of boldface for emphasis
- use of horizontal lines to emphasize text

After

Disclaimer

The holder is admitted on condition, and by use of this ticket agrees, that he will not transmit or aid in transmitting any description, account, picture or reproduction of the baseball game or exhibition to which this ticket admits him. Breach of the foregoing will automatically terminate this license.

   The holder assumes all risk and dangers incidental to the game of baseball including specifically (but not exclusively) the danger of being injured by thrown or batted balls and agrees that the participating clubs, their agents and players are not liable for injuries resulting from such causes.

   The management reserves the right to revoke the license granted by this ticket.

It matters how your document looks. You're not using a typewriter, so take advantage of the modern wisdom in document design and create a look that invites readers in and rewards them with accessibility and readability.

Drafting Conventions & Plain English

When preparing plain-English transactional documents, be aware of the risks of forms and drop the over-formal, outdated conventions of traditional legal drafting.

Using forms

Generally speaking, there are fewer forms available for plain legal drafting as compared to traditional legal drafting. So most drafters must prepare plain legal documents from scratch or from a form that contains traditional, legalese drafting. Forms save time and, therefore, money, so they're a necessity in any legal practice. But particularly for plain legal drafting, forms present some problems.

First, forms generally contain outdated and excessively formal language. The plain legal drafter's first job is to revise old-fashioned language into plain English. If the form has been used in many previous transactions, it will have the weight of precedent behind it. For the plain legal drafter, this is always a concern. If you change the form, you might risk fouling up the transaction. So when using a form, it's particularly important to make the plain-English version contain the same substance as the original form. This is why the first step in any effort to revise a traditional legal form into plain English is to take careful notes about every item of substantive content in the original. For more on the process of converting a form to plain English, see Chapter 2.

Second, forms usually contain numerous drafting inconsistencies. This is to be expected, of course, because most forms are a hodgepodge, cobbled together from a variety of sources, all of which probably had different authors. Thus the form won't speak with a consistent voice and may contain many problematic usages.

Third, forms foster an unfortunate tendency toward haste and laziness. Because it can often be quite easy to simply change the names and the dates to produce a first draft of a new document, using a form is deceptively easy. Experienced drafters know better. You must master the form and make it your own. Get familiar with every aspect of the form document. Some good news for plain legal drafters is that once you've begun drafting documents for a nonlegal audience, you'll begin to develop a source of plain-English forms.

From traditional drafting conventions to plain English

Whether you're using a form or not, when preparing plain-English legal documents, you won't need the outdated, over-formal conventions of traditional legal drafting. Instead, revise them, modernize them, or drop them.

Recitals

In traditional legal documents, the opening paragraph, which introduces the parties, is followed by a series of paragraphs that lawyers often call the "recitals." Traditional recitals typically contain a number of "whereas" paragraphs followed by a "now therefore" paragraph, like this:

Original recitals

> WHEREAS, Attorney is about to undertake the performance of substantial legal services on behalf of the Personal Representative; and
>
> WHEREAS, the State Bar's rules of professional conduct encourage attorneys and clients to enter into fee agreements; and
>
> WHEREAS, the Probate Code requires that attorney fee agreements be signed by the personal representative;

NOW THEREFORE, in consideration of their mutual promises stated herein, the parties hereby agree that:

For consumer-oriented documents written in plain English, recitals aren't mandatory. They can provide helpful background, and it might be user-friendly to set the stage and explain the context, but cutting them out entirely probably wouldn't hurt anything.

You can retain recitals as a way to introduce the document, provide a summary of the transaction, or clarify the intentions of the parties. If you do, abandon the stilted and archaic style of *whereas* and *now therefore*.

Legal-drafting expert Kenneth Adams recommends presenting the recitals in a much more simplified way in his book *A Manual of Style for Contract Drafting*.[1] Omit *whereas* and *now therefore*, and frame each recital as a separate sentence. With some other plain-English revisions, the recitals might look like this:

Better recitals

The Attorney is about to perform substantial legal services for the Personal Representative.

The State Bar's rules of professional conduct encourage attorneys and clients to have fee agreements.

The Probate Code requires that attorney fee agreements be signed by the Personal Representative.

Therefore, the parties agree as follows:

Defined terms

There are other names, but when I used the phrase "defined terms" (the "Defined Terms"), I mean exactly what I did in earlier in this sentence: I introduced a term and then made that term into a proper noun by placing it inside parentheses and quotation marks with initial capital letters.

---

[1] Kenneth A. Adams, *A Manual of Style for Contract Drafting* (3d ed. 2013).

If you're going to be a committed, plain-English drafter, you should do what you can to reduce defined terms in your documents. One way to do that is to create and use a defined term only when you'll use the term several times. In my reading of transactional documents, I'm surprised at how frequently I see a defined term created and then never used. For example, in the following text, the defined term "CPC" is introduced but never used:

> THIS PARKING PASS IS A REVOCABLE LICENSE THAT LICENSES THE HOLDER TO PARK 1 VEHICLE IN 1 PARKING SPOT AT CHERRY PARK CENTER ("CPC"), AT HOLDER'S SOLE RISK. HALL CHERRY PARK LLC, REGAN HOCKEY CLUB, THE CITY OF CHERRY PARK AND EACH OF THEIR RESPECTIVE AFFILIATES, OWNERS, AGENTS AND EMPLOYEES (COLLECTIVELY, "HCP") ASSUME NO RESPONSIBILITY FOR THEFT OR DAMAGE TO THE VEHICLE OR ANY ARTICLE LEFT IN THE VEHICLE. HOLDER HEREBY AGREES THAT HCP IS NOT LIABLE FOR INJURIES OR DAMAGES RELATED TO HOLDER'S ATTENDANCE AT SUCH GAME OR EVENT OR THE PARKING OF THE VEHICLE. HCP ASSUMES NO RESPONSIBILITY FOR LOST, STOLEN OR DESTROYED PARKING PASSES. HOLDER IS NOT ENTITLED TO A CASH REFUND OR REPLACEMENT TICKET. THIS PASS DOES NOT CREATE AN EXPRESS OR IMPLIED BAILMENT AGREEMENT.

Even if the defined term is actually used once or twice, you might still consider not creating it. You save yourself some typing, of course, but if the original term isn't long, repeating it a few times in the document won't hurt anything.

When you do create defined terms, skip the archaic or fancy conventions. Often, you can simply use the term and then put it inside parentheses with an initial capital letter.

Instead of this:

> This publishing contract is entered by Jackie Griffin (hereinafter "Griffin") and Evermore Computer Publishing House, Inc. (hereinafter "ECPHI").

Do this:
> This publishing contract is entered by Jackie Griffin (Griffin) and Evermore Computer Publishing House, Inc. (ECPHI).

And speaking of "ECPHI" (how is that pronounced?), don't create awkward acronyms or initials unnecessarily. Unless Evermore Computer Publishing House, Inc., always uses the initials ECPHI, you're better off defining it as "Evermore."

Here's the parking pass from before, with simplified defined terms (and no all-caps):

> This parking pass is a revocable license that licenses the holder to park 1 vehicle in 1 parking spot at Cherry Park Center at holder's sole risk. Hall Cherry Park LLC, Regan Hockey Club, the City of Cherry Park and each of their respective affiliates, owners, agents and employees ("Hall") assume no responsibility for theft or damage to the vehicle or any article left in the vehicle. Holder hereby agrees that Hall is not liable for injuries or damages related to holder's attendance at such game or event or the parking of the vehicle. Hall assumes no responsibility for lost, stolen or destroyed parking passes. Holder is not entitled to a cash refund or replacement ticket. This pass does not create an express or implied bailment agreement.

To take plain English even further, let's acknowledge that when you create a defined term for a person or corporation, it's sometimes acceptable to omit the parentheses and quotation marks entirely if there's only one person or entity with that name. Old-school transactional drafters may balk at this convention, but it works:

> This publishing contract is entered by Jackie Griffin and Evermore Computer Publishing House, Inc. Griffin and Evermore have agreed that Griffin will write and Evermore will publish a book aimed at the technology market.

This convention is simple, and it's the way other professionals write. Ask yourself if you've ever seen a newspaper or magazine article that looks like this:

> When local teacher and author Jackie Griffin ("Griffin") wanted to publish her book on technical writing, she first tried to go with a local publisher like Evermore Computer Publishing House, Inc. ("Evermore").

No. Avoiding that awkward convention is appropriate for plain legal drafting, too. Again, if there's only one Griffin and one Evermore in the document, so ambiguity won't result, creating defined terms isn't strictly necessary.

Definitions

Another drafting convention is definitions, creating meanings for words. I have two recommendations for definitions.

First, you should never begin a consumer document with a lengthy definitions section. This convention may be acceptable for sophisticated transactional lawyers, but it's counterproductive and off-putting to everyday readers. Experts on drafting, such as Kenneth Adams, suggest that a lengthy definitions section belongs at the end of the document, not the beginning.

Second, use the word *means* and almost nothing else to introduce a definition. Don't use any of these:

> "Business Day" shall mean …
> "Business Day" shall have the following meaning …
> "Business Day" will have the following meaning …

Instead, use this:

> "Business Day" means …

Words of obligation

In any kind of binding legal text—contracts, wills, trusts, rules, regulations, and statutes—you'll need to impose obligations on someone. You'll need to state the duties.

In traditional transactional drafting, the most common word used to impose obligations is *shall*. Although it's often used mistakenly for the future tense, or simply to give a document a musty odor, its correct use is to impose a legal duty on the actor in a sentence, like this:

The Buyer shall pay ...

- means the Buyer has a duty to pay

You shall submit a completed application ...

- means you are required to submit a completed application

The Lender shall provide notice ...

- means the Lender has a contractual obligation to provide notice

Whether *shall* is the right word to use to impose an obligation in traditional transactional documents is an open question. But according to Joseph Kimble, who even wrote an article called *The Many Misuses of Shall*,[2] it's certainly not the right word to use in a plain-English document. Avoid *shall* in plain-English drafting.

What are your other choices? You have several:

will

- When you use *will* in binding legal text, it indicates a promise to do something. In using *will*, be careful to use it only for promises. In other words, *The Landlord will maintain the property* is proper because the Landlord is promising. But *The Lease will expire on July 1* is poor because it indicates mere future tense. Better to write *The Lease expires on July 1* and reserve *will* for promises.

agree to

---

2. 3 Scribes J. Legal Writing 61 (1992).

50 Plain Legal Writing: Do It

- When you use *agree to* in binding legal text, it indicates the party's assent to the obligation. This is another way of saying that the party promises.

promise to
- When you use *promise to* in binding legal text, it indicates a promise to do something.

must
- When you use *must* in binding legal text, it imposes an obligation on the party.

For plain legal drafting, I prefer to use *agree to* or *will*. Both are short, clear, and relatively unambiguous. I generally avoid *must* for two reasons: *must* can seem bossy; and *must* could be reserved for imposing a condition, rather than a mere promise.

Once you've decided what word or phrase to use, scan the document carefully to locate and properly frame the obligations. This means deciding which party has the obligation and what the obligation entails. In doing this, you should impose all obligations in the same language. Inconsistency in the language of obligations is sloppy, confusing, and risky. For example, I routinely encounter single documents in which the obligations are imposed in a variety of ways:

Buyer agrees to ...
Buyer shall ...
Buyer further agrees to ...
Buyer expressly agrees to ...
Buyer must ...

And so on. This is confusing and unnecessary. Pick one phrase for imposing obligations and stick with it.

Words of discretion
Just as you should be consistent in the language of obligation, you should be consistent in the language of discretion. The general and most basic word of discretion is *may*. If I say you "may" do

something, this means you have permission to do it. Unfortunately, the word *may* also means *might* or *possibly*. To avoid this potential ambiguity, you have two choices.

First, you could use *may* but limit it to one meaning. When you intend to give a party permission, use *may*, and only *may*, using no other words to give permission. Then, when you want to indicate a possibility, use *might*. With this approach, you must use scrupulous care to avoid ever using *may* to mean a possibility. For example:

The Tenant may paint interior walls.

- This is a correct use of *may* for giving permission.

Tenant's use of unapproved paint colors may result in a deduction from the deposit.

- This is a use of *may* to mean *might*. Ideally, you would limit *may* to a single meaning (permission) and use another word here, such as *might* or *could*.

Second, you could choose to use a phrase in place of *may* when you intend to give an actor permission. With this approach, you could then use *may* for possibilities, as long as you never use it for granting permission. Possible permission phrases include

- has a right to
- has authority to
- has permission to

The keys for using words of permission are twofold: always be sure you know whether you are granting permission or describing a possibility; and never use one word, such as *may*, to mean both.

Presenting numbers

In plain legal drafting, we abandon the tradition of doubling up numerals and text. So we don't write this:

Seller must give notice within thirty (30) days.

And we definitely don't write this:

52 Plain Legal Writing: Do It

> The purchase price is FIFTY THOUSAND AND NO 100s DOLLARS ($50,000).

This is asking for trouble. Although doubling up the numerals and text might, as some have suggested, force you to double-check your figures, it also presents twice as many opportunities to make mistakes. Pick one expression of the number (probably numerals) and stick with it.

Synonym strings

In plain legal drafting, we do all we can to avoid unnecessary doublets, triplets, and synonym strings. I can't possibly list for you every synonym string used in legal drafting with a plain-English substitute, but here's a start:

Instead of this	**Try this**
interpreted, construed, and governed by	governed by
power and authority	power
right, title, and interest	interest
sell, convey, assign, and transfer	sell

In general, you can go through three steps when attacking legalistic synonym strings.

1. Ask yourself: Are any words in the string redundant? Use a dictionary. Use a legal-usage dictionary. Then delete any redundant words.
2. Now ask yourself: Of the remaining, nonredundant words, do you need them all? In other words, do you need all these different meanings? If you don't, delete the words whose meanings you don't need.
3. If you still have more than one word remaining, ask yourself: Is there a single word that would cover all the

meanings you need? If so, use it. If not, keep the remaining string.

Here's an example of a four-word string:

Original

The holder will not transmit any description, account, picture, or reproduction of the baseball game.

1. Are any of these words redundant?
   - Yes, *description* and *account* are redundant, or at least redundant enough that we can eliminate one of them.
2. Do we need all the following meanings: description, picture, and reproduction?
   - No. I'll be bold and take the position that we don't need the word *reproduction*. For me, it's included within the meanings of *description* and *picture*.
3. Is there a single word that will cover all the meanings we need?
   - No. To me, the word *description* covers the audio, and the word *picture* covers the visual. I think we need both.

Revision

The holder will not transmit any description or picture of the baseball game.

Provisos

Phrases and clauses tacked on with *provided, provided that, provided however that,* and *provided further that* are, as *Garner's Dictionary of Legal Usage* puts it, "a reliable signal that the draft is not going well."[3] Although you'll need to cut many traditional

---

3. Bryan A. Garner, *Garner's Dictionary of Legal Usage* 727 (2011).

drafting phrases in a plain legal document (see Chapter 8), provisos are so frequent they merit special attention.

The problem, besides their archaic flavor and their tendency to perplex the ordinary reader, is that they're vague. They can create exceptions, conditions, and additions, according to Garner. Instead, say what you mean with a precise term rather than rely on a vague proviso. Often, the proviso language can be deleted.

Before

> Insured assigns to Insurer all rights and claims the Insured may have against any person or entity who may be liable for the loss or injury resulting from the occurrence above described; provided, however, that this assignment is limited to an amount equal to the amount of benefits paid to the Insured by Insurer with respect to the loss or injury.

After

> Insured assigns Insurer all rights and claims the Insured may have against any person or entity who may be liable for the loss or injury resulting from the occurrence above described. This assignment is limited to an amount equal to the amount of benefits paid to the Insured by Insurer with respect to the loss or injury.

Ambiguous modifiers

Traditional drafting sometimes causes confusion through leading and trailing modifiers. A leading modifier appears before a list and could apply only to the first or to all the items. For example:

> The trustees may provide funds to charitable schools, hospitals, and institutions.

- Does *charitable* modify only *schools*, so that the trustees may fund charitable schools but any hospitals and institutions? Or does charitable modify schools, hospitals, and institutions?

To fix the ambiguity of the leading modifier, you must know what you mean. If you mean that only the schools must be charitable, you can place the modifier directly before the item it modifies and then place that item last:

> The trustees may provide funds to hospitals, institutions, and charitable schools.

If you mean schools, hospitals, and institutions must all be charitable, you have two options. You can repeat the modifier:

> The trustees may provide funds to charitable schools, charitable hospitals, and charitable institutions.

It's wordy but clear. Or you can tabulate (place each item on its own line) and create a numbered or lettered list:

> The trustees may provide funds to charitable
> a. schools,
> b. hospitals, and
> c. institutions.

If you want the leading modifier to apply to every item in the list, tabulating is a good solution. When in doubt, make a list.

A trailing modifier appears after a list or series and presents ambiguity about whether it applies only to the last item in the list or to all items. For example, a statute requires a city to maintain "highways." The word "highway" is defined to include:

> ... bridges, sidewalks, trailways, crosswalks, and *culverts on the highway*.[4]

- Does the phrase *on the highway* modify only *culverts*, so that for culverts, a city must maintain only those that are on a highway but must maintain all bridges, sidewalks, trailways, and crosswalks (a sizeable duty)? Or does the phrase *on the highway* modify all

---

4. Thomas Myers, *Clearing up Ambiguity from a Series Modifier*, Mich. B.J. 52 (Nov. 2011) (emphasis added).

the items, so that a city must maintain only those bridges, sidewalks, trailways, crosswalks, and culverts that are on a highway (a much smaller duty)?

To fix the ambiguity of the trailing modifier, you must know what you mean. If you mean that only the culverts must be on a highway, you can place the modifier directly after the item to be modified and place that item first, like this:

"Highway" ... includes culverts on the highway, bridges, sidewalks, trailways, and crosswalks.

If you mean all the items must be on the highway, you have two options. You can include clarifying language before the list:

"Highway" ... includes all the following on the highway: bridges, sidewalks, trailways, crosswalks, and culverts.

Or you can tabulate, creating a numbered or lettered list:

"Highway" ... includes all the following on the highway:
a. bridges,
b. sidewalks,
c. trailways,
d. crosswalks, and
e. culverts.

Both types of ambiguous modifiers discussed here are easy to fix; the key is recognizing them as you draft.

So whether you're drafting from scratch or using a form, don't let outdated and ambiguous conventions of traditional legal drafting survive in your plain-English document.

Organization & Signposts

In plain-English documents, put key information, or a summary, right up front. Use a sensible large-scale organization, and use headings, subheadings, and numbering to cue small-scale organization.

Your goal is always to make your document easy to read, but if the document is longer than a few pages (or in some cases, longer than a few paragraphs), it's just as important to make the document easy to skim. Why? Because your readers are busy—as busy as you are—and you're not being honest with yourself if you think they'll all read your document from beginning to end.

So it should be as easy to skim the document as it is to read it straight through. It should also be easy to skip around in your document. By adopting those goals and acknowledging that few will read your document from beginning to end, you can better organize and signpost the document. This chapter offers several techniques for ordering and signposting your plain-English document with techniques for titles and advice for numbering.

The title of your document

Give your document a short but descriptive title. You should aim to convey descriptive and distinguishing information with the fewest number of words. That's why short, one-word titles usually won't do:

58 Plain Legal Writing: Do It

> Agreement
> Disclosure

These titles are too abstract; they tell the reader almost nothing about the document's content. Yet these more-descriptive titles are needlessly long:

> Attorney and Executor Agreement on Legal Representation for the Probate Estate of Jefferson T. Gladwell, deceased

> One- and Three-month Cost-of-Funds Indexed Option Adjustable Rate Mortgage Disclosure Statement

Be descriptive but not wordy:

> Agreement to Hire a Probate Attorney

As a compromise between long and short titles, a subtitle can help:

> Disclosure Statement for Your Loan
>
> One- and Three-month Cost-of-Funds Indexed Option ARM

Once you've picked a good title, put it in a larger type size and use boldface. As recommended in Chapter 2, you might also put the title in a contrasting font: if the body text is serifed (and it probably should be), then the title (and even the main topic headings) could be in a sans serif font.

> Interest Rate and Loan Fee Policy
> Pricing Package Agreement
> This agreement allows you to lock in the interest rate (and other terms) for your loan, so you can know what interest rate you'll pay at closing, and you can avoid the risk that rates might rise. The items you lock in are called your Pricing Package.

And consider placement: A left-aligned title will enhance the left-aligned feel of the document, especially if all the headings are on the left margin, too. Left alignment eases skimming. But a centered title is traditional and entirely appropriate. A right-aligned title makes it easier to see the titles when leafing through a number of documents.

Large-scale organization—the up-front summary

When you're planning and creating the large-scale organization of your document, you're choosing and ordering the major parts. In doing so, keep two questions in mind.

First, what's the most important information in the document? In a persuasive document, the most important information is the result you seek, with reasons. In a demand letter, the most important information is the demand. In an opinion letter, the most important information is the opinion. For transactional, plain-English documents, the most important information might not be one of the substantive terms; rather, it is probably a summary of the transaction or a statement of its purpose.

Second, where should you place the most important information? All legal writing should begin with an up-front summary of the most important information, whether it's a preview, a thesis, or a mini-outline. So the first part of your large-scale organization is the up-front summary. This chapter treats up-front summaries in transactional, plain-English documents. For a discussion of up-front summaries in analytical documents aimed at nonlawyers, see Chapter 6.

Preparing an up-front summary in a transactional document can be tricky. As Joseph Kimble noted: "[W]hen it comes to the field that we call drafting—contracts, wills, trusts, statutes, rules, and the like—the summary will not encapsulate the analysis because there is no analysis. Rather, the summary will take the form of an introduction or overview."[1] So in a transactional document, explain what the document does and why the reader should read it.

Martin Cutts, the author of the *Oxford Guide to Plain English*, says you should "organize your material in a way that helps

---

1. Joseph Kimble, *First Things First: The Lost Art of Summarizing*. 8 Scribes J. Leg. Writing 103, 114 (2001–2002).

readers to grasp the important information early and to navigate through the document easily."[2] I agree.

For example, consider these three up-front summaries for transactional documents used in a plain-English project for a bank. The originals had included no up-front summaries:

> This disclosure statement explains the one- and three-month COFI Option ARM loans.
>
> This document contains notices and disclosures that are part of the loan application.
>
> This agreement allows you to lock in the interest rate (and other terms) for your loan, so you can know what interest rate you'll pay, and you can avoid the risk that rates might rise. The items you lock in are called your Pricing Package.

As you can see, the length of and detail in an up-front summary will vary, depending on the length of and detail in the document.

A final note on up-front summaries: even though the summary appears first in the document, you usually can't write it first. You should do at least one draft of the entire document first. Only then will you know what belongs in the summary.

Large-scale organization—ordering

After the up-front summary, you have several options in ordering the rest of the document:

- Order of importance
- Topical order
- Order by party obligations
- Order by tradition
- Chronological order

I generally recommend arranging the main parts of a document in the order of their importance. Nearly all readers pay more attention at the beginning of the document, so it makes sense to put

---

2. Martin Cutts, *Oxford Guide to Plain English* xxxi (4 ed. 2013).

the most important information there and then descend to the least important information.

After order of importance, I recommend trying to order by topics in a logical way. Choose your topics and put them in an order that makes logical sense to you. Of course, paradoxically, the best way to test whether your own order is logical is to ask someone else to assess it.

Next, consider ordering by obligation. I have on occasion recommended that my students try ordering a bilateral contract by the parties' obligations. With this approach, part one of the document is a summary, part two of the document lists all the obligations of one party, and part three lists all the obligations of the other party. The remaining parts of the document follow. This approach to ordering, which is highly unconventional in traditional transactional drafting, is reader-friendly. If the parties actually read the document, they can find all their obligations in one place.

Ordering by party obligation makes things easy for the reader, but it is certainly more challenging for the drafter. Typical transactional documents are ordered based on the order of the original form—what I call ordering by tradition. This is acceptable, but a traditional order is usually writer focused, not reader focused.

Chronological order is not a common ordering convention in legal drafting.

Small-scale organization of the document

Once you've titled the document, placed your summary up front, and ordered the main parts, you should connect those parts with small-scale organization techniques. I think of small-scale organization as having three main components:

1. Headings
2. Numbering
3. Topic and transition sentences

I discuss each here.

Headings

Headings come in two varieties. These are the first type—topic headings:

> Loan Payments
> Arbitration
> Buyer's Duties

Notice that these short topic headings use initial capitals and no punctuation—standard practices for traditional and plain-English drafting.

Short topic headings can be expanded into the second type of heading—explanatory or sentence-length headings, also called point headings, like these:

> Paying back your loan
> You must arbitrate disputes before suing in court.
> The buyer's duties under this contract

Notice that explanatory headings use sentence capitalization (first word) and take a period when the heading is a complete sentence.

The best practice is to keep all headings at the same level consistent and in the same style. So, for example, all the major headings would be a single word or a short phrase, would identify a topic, and would use initial capitals and no punctuation. All the first-level subheadings would be complete sentences, would briefly explain or summarize the content, and would use sentence capitalization with a period.

Generally, I like to use topic headings for major parts of the document and explanatory headings for smaller parts such as subsections and paragraphs. The following example shows how topic headings and subheadings might appear in a plain-English document.

> **Background**
> You've asked me to administer the probate estate of [Name]. You are the representative. In administering the estate, I'll be

performing legal services for you, and you'll pay me for my time and expenses....

Terms
I charge an hourly fee.
You'll pay me $175 per hour for attorney time and $85 per hour for paralegal time for all time my paralegals and I spend administering the estate....

There's a limit on my fee.
I won't bill you for ordinary services that exceed the percentages allowed by state law, but I can bill you for extraordinary services that exceed those limits....

I'll bill you monthly.
I'll bill you monthly for fees and expenses, and at that time you'll pay me from the estate's assets....

I won't be charging the statutory fees.
State law provides for default fees of $1,500 for the first $40,000 of the estate, plus $750 for the next $30,000 of the estate, plus $750 for the next $30,000 of the estate, plus 3% of the remaining value of the estate for attorney services....

One additional type of heading format is the inline heading or the run-in heading. It gives you another level of headings and takes up less space. It looks like this:

Hourly fee. You'll pay me $175 per hour for attorney time and $85 per hour for paralegal time for all time my paralegals and I spend administering the estate...

Fee limit. I won't bill you for ordinary services that exceed the percentages allowed by state law, but I can bill you for extraordinary services that exceed those limits....

Monthly billing. I'll bill you monthly for fees and expenses, and at that time you'll pay me from the estate's assets....

You have many options, but here's an approach to headings I recommend:

Title (large)	large, boldface, sans serif font
Main headings	regular size, boldface, sans-serif font
Subheadings and inline headings	regular size, boldface, serifed font (same font as main text)
Lower-level subheadings (bold italic)	regular size, bold italics, serifed font (same font as main text)
Lower-level subheadings	regular size, italics, serifed font (same font as main text)

You need not use all these levels in every document, and you may choose among them for any particular document. Even in a long document, three or four levels would be enough. In practice, the document would look like this:

Title

You may or may not have text directly below the title, before the body of the document. Often you will, because this is a good place for the up-front summary or overview.

Main headings

The main headings, in a boldface, sans serif font, contrast strongly with the body text and stand out, making them easy to see and skim.

Subheadings

Subheadings, in the same font as the main text, stand out because they are in boldface.

Sub-subheadings or sub-subheadings

These use bold italics or merely italics, giving you options for two additional levels.

Inline headings. The inline heading, even though it is the same size as the subheading, is obviously the lowest level of the hierarchy because it is in the same line as the opening line of the text.

One more comment about headings: if the previous example were a real document, I might have suggested to the author that it has too many headings. Just as too few headings can leave the reader swimming in a sea of undifferentiated text, too many headings can create a busy, cluttered appearance , chopping the document up and making it harder to skim.

Numbering

Most transactional documents need comprehensive numbering. Plain-English documents may or may not—comprehensive numbering could add formality you don't want. But if you apply a numbering system to your document, choose a sensible system and try not to leave dangling (unnumbered) text. In addition, unlike headings, not all numbered provisions need to be left aligned—moderate tabbing can enhance readability. But whatever you do, always use proper alignment (see Chapter 3).

Even if the document is comprehensively numbered, you need not over-apply numbering. In other words, you need not tabulate (put each item on its own line) and number every list. Just as it's possible to have too many headings in the document, it's also possible to have too much numbering. Novices, enamored of numbering as a way to reduce imprecision, sometimes get carried away:

  2. Monthly Bills
 (A) The Attorney will bill fees, and
 (B) the Personal Representative will pay the fees out of the assets of the Estate monthly.
 (C) The Personal Representative will also pay expenses monthly.
 (D) Expenses include
 (1) copies,
 (2) postage,
 (3) filing fees, and
 (4) other items.

This provision could be just as easily rendered without numbering and, because of flow, would actually be easier to read:

> 2. Monthly Bills
> The Attorney will bill fees, and the Personal Representative will pay the fees out of the assets of the Estate monthly. The Personal Representative will also pay expenses monthly. Expenses include copies, postage, filing fees, and other items.

Many consumer-oriented, transactional documents are not as formal and do not need comprehensive numbering. Generally speaking, strong, skimmable headings are enough, with occasional numbering for subparts and sequential lists.

Numbering systems

Choose a sensible numbering system. For more guidance, see Chapter 3.

Topic and transition sentences

Topic and transition sentences have little or no role in transactional plain-English documents. Rather, the topics and transitions are cued with headings and numbering in transactional documents. But using topic and transition sentences in a plain-English analytical document such as a brief, a memo, or a letter is important.

Other organizational aids

You can make your documents easy to read and easy to skim with two other organizational aids: a table of contents and a glossary.

Table of contents

I don't have a hard-and-fast rule, but when a single document stretches onto a fifth page, I always consider providing a table of contents near the beginning. You can use a traditional table of contents, or it can be informal, like this:

> This document has 4 parts:
> 1. Locking in your Pricing Package

2. Prepayment fees and reduced-documentation loans
3. Terms that apply to all options
4. Information about fees

Glossary

Rather than loading the front of your document with a long section of definitions, consider including a glossary at the end of the document. The glossary might include definitions for all defined terms in the document and could do double duty as an index, allowing readers to find key terms in the text.

Nearly all traditional transactional documents are ordered and organized for the ease of the writer. In plain-English drafting, we focus instead on the ease of the reader. The ideal plain-English document uses the techniques in this chapter to make the document easy to read and easy to skim.

Plain Letters & Email

> When writing correspondence in plain English, get to the point early and be human.

No matter your practice, you'll write letters and email messages to nonlawyers at some point. In some practice areas, you'll do it a lot. When corresponding with nonlawyers, you must balance your desire to sound professional with your need to communicate. It's tricky, and some lawyers lean too far to the "sound professional" end of the spectrum. This is too bad.

Let your knowledge of the law and your ability to communicate clearly show your professionalism. Don't take the misguided approach of thinking you'll impress the nonlawyer with a formal and legalistic style. Instead, when corresponding with nonlawyers, adopt a conversational tone.

But before we talk about tone, let's begin with beginnings.

Up-front summary

All communication with nonlawyers should begin with an up-front summary of some kind—a theme of several chapters in this book. It's the courteous thing to do, and it communicates much more effectively than beginning with background. In other words, yes—it's okay to spoil the ending.

The advice to begin a legal letter or email message with an up-front summary is black-letter law; no one says different:

70 Plain Legal Writing: Do It

> By establishing the main points of a document before launching into a detailed analysis of these points, you show readers what information to look for.[1]

> I have run across [those] who thought this was the way to write reports: Feed out details gradually, "create suspense," save the big news to the last. But this is a poor way to organize a piece of writing that is chiefly information.[2]

> [K]nowing where a discussion or argument is heading is essential if a reader is to understand on first reading.[3]

> I know of only one good reason for saving big news till the end— deliberate obfuscation ...[4]

Yet too many letters and email messages directed at nonlawyers begin with vague background, abstractions, or—worst of all— tedious factual details such as party names and dates. This was the case with a collection letter I ran across:

> On January 31, 2005, WyTech Sales, Inc. (the "Borrower") entered into an agreement with Nuttall Systems & Technology Transfer, Inc. ("NSTT") under which all of the Borrower's accounts receivable ("Receivables") of which you are the obligor have been pledged to NSTT. The Borrower has established a lockbox (the "Lockbox") for collection of Receivables. Accordingly, you are hereby instructed to remit all payments of Receivables of which you are, or have been, the obligor to ...

Think about how this letter begins. Frankly, the date of the agreement and even the agreement itself are background details at best and irrelevant to the reader at worst. Why not begin with an

---

1. Frederic G. Gale & Joseph M. Moxley, *How to Write the Winning Brief* 107 (1992).
2. Robert Gunning, *The Technique of Clear Writing* 130 (1968).
3. Lynn B. Squires, Marjorie Dick Rombauer & Katherine See Kennedy, *Legal Writing in a Nutshell* 32–33 (2d ed. 1996).
4. Martin Cutts, *Oxford Guide to Plain English* 134 (2004).

introductory summary? Even a single sentence will do; then get to the background:

> This letter contains instructions for you to begin paying accounts you owe WyTech Sales, Inc. to Nuttall Systems & Technology Transfer, Inc.

That's the way to begin an important letter containing important instructions. Good writers begin their correspondence, whether letters or email messages, with an up-front summary on nearly every occasion. The only exceptions, truly, are personal messages and very short correspondence.

For example, all the following openers would work well for plain-English documents; each reflects the writer's effort to communicate so as to ease the reader's way:

When giving advice or an opinion:

> You've asked if you must tell your medical patients that you receive incentives from their HMOs if you withhold certain medical services. We've concluded that although no specific law requires you to disclose the incentives, you should disclose them to avoid any possible liability.

- Notice that the opening paragraph of this letter frames the issue briefly and gives a short answer, supported by a general reason. A fuller statement of the issue with the facts, the detailed answer, and the specific reasons would follow in the body of the letter.

When making a demand:

> This firm represents First Federal Credit Union. You owe $2,250 for a signature loan and related fees. Full payment is due now.

- Resist the urge to begin a demand or settlement letter with legal or factual background. Resist the urge to build your case line by line and then place the specific demand at the end. Accept the fact that even though you're concerned about shocking the reader with an

72 Plain Legal Writing: Do It

up-front dollar amount, if you hide the dollar amount at the end of the letter, your reader will inevitably look there first anyway.

When giving instructions:

This letter outlines the four steps you'll need to take to secure the mechanic's lien on the Litchfield property.
1. ...
2. ...

- Notice that summaries do not always need to contain a lot of detail. It might be enough to simply preview what and how much information is coming. And if you tell the reader there are four things coming, why not number them?

When seeking information:

Who in our company is the appropriate person to sit for a deposition in the Anderson case? You may need some background to answer that, so here it is.

- It's a natural tendency to want to give the background before the question. So this email message might typically have begun with background about the deposition or the case. That might work when you're speaking, but in writing, stating the question—the point of the message—first will allow the reader to better understand the background.

Strive to begin your letters and email messages with a summary or the point.

Conversational tone

After providing an up-front summary, the most important thing you can do in correspondence is adopt a conversational tone. Adopting a conversational tone doesn't mean writing exactly the way you speak. For most of us, our speech is far too informal, slangy, and fragmented to work well in legal correspondence. Rather, a conversational tone is one that is natural, simple, and clear. Even though it doesn't perfectly reflect your speech, you'd be comfortable speaking the words you're writing.

For example, you should feel free to use the first- and second-person pronouns *I* and *you* and the plural first-person pronouns *we* and *us*. These will give the message immediacy and personal appeal, and they'll allow you to greatly simplify the writing.

You should also feel free to use contractions when corresponding. It's fine.

But you should probably direct most of your effort to use a natural and conversational tone to diction or word choice. When you have a choice between two words, one formal and one informal, choose the informal word. When you have a choice between a legal word and an everyday-English word, choose the everyday-English word. And when you have a choice between a long word and a short word, choose the short word.

Of course, your choice shouldn't override the need for precision and accuracy. All I'm asking you to do is abandon unnecessary legalisms, formalisms, and archaic words. Consider again the opening paragraph of our collection letter, which, by the way, was sent to a nonlawyer. Following each bracketed number, you'll encounter a legalism, a tone problem, or a word-choice problem:

> On January 31, 2005, WyTech Sales, Inc. (the "Borrower") [1] entered into an agreement with Nuttall Systems & Technology Transfer, Inc. [2] ("NSTT") under which all of the Borrower's accounts receivable [3] ("Receivables") of which you are the [4] obligor have been [5] pledged to NSTT. The Borrower has established a lockbox [6] (the "Lockbox") for collection of Receivables. [7] Accordingly, you are [8] hereby instructed to [9] remit all payments of Receivables of which you are, or have been, the obligor to ...

Let's tackle these one at a time.
1. The phrase "entered into an agreement" is a nominalization—a verb that's been converted into noun form. We could shorten this to "agreed."

2. The initials "NSTT" are not a major problem, but it's possible to shorten the name of this entity simply to "Nuttall," isn't it? Now, if this company routinely refers to itself as "NSTT," you should use the initials. If not, use "Nuttall."
3. To define accounts receivable as "Receivables" is not necessary unless there are other possible receivables in the letter that might cause confusion. Simply mention "accounts receivable" and from then on refer to them as "receivables" or even "accounts."
4. How many nonlawyers are going to understand the term "obligor"? Not many. We probably can't find a one-word replacement, though. You'll see how I handle this in the rewrite.
5. Few nonlawyers are going to understand the term "pledged." Lawyers understand that this means the borrower has given Nuttall a security interest in the receivables. Maybe we could say that. Or maybe we could say that they've been given as collateral.
6. If there's only one lockbox in this letter, you don't need to create a defined term.
7. "Accordingly" is a heavy transition word, and when striving for a conversational tone you should probably prefer "and" or "so."
8. Don't use archaic terms such as "hereby" in a letter to a nonlawyer. Leave them out.
9. The phrase "remit all payments" is not only a nominalization; it also contains the fancy word "remit." We can use "pay."

Suppose you'd been given the original collection letter as a form document to use in preparing your own collection letter. As you can see, you would've needed to make extensive changes if you wanted it to actually be read and understood by a nonlawyer. Now that we've identified at least nine concerns in the letter, let's see if we can fix them:

> This letter contains instructions for you to begin paying accounts you owe WyTech Sales, Inc. to Nuttall Systems & Technology Transfer, Inc.
>
> **Background**
> On January 31, 2005, WyTech Sales, Inc., the borrower, gave Nuttall all its accounts receivable as collateral. You are the payer on some of these accounts. From now on, pay those accounts to a lockbox the borrower has established here: ...

Generally, this is a clearer and plainer message. Yes, it's still a bit legal-sounding, but that's to be expected because it affects legal rights and duties. But it's accessible and even human. And did you notice the heading? It distinctly separates the summary from the body of the letter, allowing a busy reader to skim.

Perhaps someone reading this has expertise in collections of this sort and is screaming that I've altered the legal effect of this letter in some way. I grant that as a possibility. But I say that's a problem with my legal knowledge, not a problem with plain English or with using a conversational tone in a letter.

Even though the original tone was not particularly hostile, it was legalistic and formal. In reality, you'd like the person receiving this letter to cooperate voluntarily and begin directing account payments to the lockbox. You're more likely to get the recipient's cooperation with a natural, nonlegal tone than you are with a formal, legalistic tone.

Here's another example:

Original

> You have requested this firm provide Great Mountain Homeowners Association, Inc. (the "Association") with a legal opinion regarding whether Section 4.02 of the Association's Bylaws requires a candidate to receive a majority of the votes cast at an annual meeting in order to be properly elected to the Board of Directors.

The answer to this request was in the next-to-last paragraph of the original letter.

Revision

> You've asked us to give Great Mountain Homeowners Association a legal opinion on Section 4.02 of the Association's Bylaws. Specifically, for election to the Board of Directors, does section 4.02 require a candidate to receive a majority of the votes cast at an annual meeting, or is it enough that the candidate received more votes than the next competing candidate?
>
> **Summary**
> Although long-standing Association practice has been to seat candidates who received more votes than the next competing candidate—and that practice may be legal—it would be safer to conduct a run-off election for the contested seat.

This revision uses a more natural tone and includes an up-front summary—the answer to the question posed—with a heading to signal it.

A final point to consider for opinion or advice letters: most nonlegal readers won't appreciate or understand legal citations. Generally, avoid legal citations in a letter to a nonlawyer. Of course, you could cut the legal citations from the main text and paste them into footnotes, but that might add to the formality of the document, or it might distract the reader. Whatever you do, please don't do as a lawyer told me he routinely does: "I like to leave the legal citations in there because it intimidates them a little bit. When they're a little intimidated, they realize they need me." If your law practice depends on intimidating your clients so they need you, good luck.

Formatting and layout

For general guidance on designing legal documents, see the advice in Chapter 3 on document design. The following is some specific guidance for letters and email.

Format letters and email messages in block-paragraph style—that is, with no tabs in the first line of each paragraph and with an extra space between paragraphs. Because most letters are single-spaced, standard margins (1 inch) and default type sizes can make the letter look crowded. Increase the type size and push the margins in.

Don't fear headings. Any letter that fills two pages could probably benefit from headings; they allow the reader to skim and skip. You can also make the document more accessible by using numbering for sequential information and by using bullets for emphasizing lists.

Advice for emailing nonlawyers

When corresponding with nonlawyers by email, be wise. Always think first. If you send a client legal advice in an email message, the client can forward the message with one click and destroy the privileged nature of the communication.

Use the subject line thoughtfully. As much as possible, given the space constraints, think summary, not topic. When replying or forwarding, change the subject line as appropriate. Your readers will appreciate it.

Keep the length of client emails short. No one likes to read long email messages. If you need to write a long message, consider writing a letter instead.

Be professional and polite. In your role as a lawyer, it's probably best to use a salutation (Dear Joan,) and a signoff (Sincerely,). But they need not be that formal. You could greet the reader informally (Joan,) and close informally too (Take care,).

You can't write to nonlawyers the way you write to opposing counsel or your colleagues. You've got to simplify. Your goal should be to sound natural and conversational. If this means you don't sound like a lawyer, even better.

Plain-English Words

> To draft plainly, nix foreign words, archaic words, legal jargon, and dispensable terms of art. Explain indispensable legal words. Favor the crisp, the natural, and the personal.

This chapter covers the most controversial aspect in all of plain-English writing: words. For the most part, words are what make legal language sound legal. More than our documents, more than our paragraphs, and more than our sentences, our words set us apart as lawyers. Simplify the words, and the text sounds like regular English. So when I tell lawyers to change their words—to simplify them—I'm almost telling them to change their identities. That's a problem for some lawyers.

Lawyers are smart and often well read. We're used to reading and using tough vocabulary. We're capable of handling the big words and the legal terminology, so some of us wonder why we should simplify. We've worked hard to master the specialized language we call legal English, and we don't want to limit ourselves.

But let's be clear: to write plainly you don't need to limit your own vocabulary or your own understanding of words. In fact, the larger your vocabulary, the better a writer you're likely to be. As Rudolf Flesch said, you just have to use the right words at the right times and places:

> So if you have a big vocabulary and know a lot of rare and fancy words, that's fine. Be proud of your knowledge. It's important in

reading and in learning. But when it comes to using your vocabulary, don't throw those big words around where they don't belong. They are handy for writing formal letters and essays or for scientific and scholarly discussions. Also for solving crossword puzzles. But they're not good for informal use....

It's a good rule to know as many rare words as possible for your reading, but to use as few of them as possible in your writing.[1]

In this chapter, I'll first introduce five types of words that aren't right for plain legal drafting: Latin and French, archaic words, legalese and jargon, terms of art, and hyperformal words. Then I'll suggest some words that will make your text crisp, natural, and personal.

Latin and French

Generally speaking, do everything you can to avoid using Latin and French in documents for nonlawyers. If you're preparing a document for an audience of lawyers, that's a different matter. You might choose to avoid Latin and French, and I think that's wise. But in a document for nonlawyers, you should never use a phrases like *cestui que trust*, *sua sponte*, or *inter alia*. Even unavoidable Latin terms of art (*de novo*, *ex parte*, *habeas corpus*) should appear only as a last resort and be defined when used.

Archaic words

Avoid obviously archaic terms. They have no place in drafting for nonlawyers. In every case, there are plain-English equivalents. For example, in a contract for representation of a professional athlete, I found all of these archaic words:

    hereinafter
    hereof
    hereto
    hereunder
    in witness whereof

---

1. Rudolf Flesch, *How to Write Better* 25, 35 (1951).

> thereof
> therein
> witnesseth

These words make the contract, which was signed in 2004, sound as if it were written in 1804.

In the case of archaic *here-* and *there-* words such as *hereof* and *thereof*, you have simple substitutes available: *this agreement* or *that agreement*. Here's a before-and-after version of a paragraph from the representation contract with the archaic terms highlighted:

Before—with archaic words

> Player shall reimburse Contract Advisor for all reasonable and necessary travel expenses actually incurred by Contract Advisor during the term **hereof** in the negotiation of Player's contract, but only if such expenses and approximate amounts **thereof** shall be approved in advance by Player.

And here's a version with everyday-English words instead.

After—with everyday English

> Player shall reimburse Contract Advisor for all reasonable and necessary travel expenses actually incurred by Contract Advisor during the term **of this agreement** in the negotiation of Player's contract, but only if such expenses and approximate amounts **of those expenses** shall be approved in advance by Player.

Yes, the everyday English version takes more words than the archaic version. That's a natural and sometimes unavoidable consequence of converting legal text into language a nonlawyer can understand. Don't worry; most of the time you'll more than make up for the excess words by shortening other parts.

The archaic words from this contract aren't the only archaic words worth eliminating. There are lots more. Some others:

> aforesaid
> be it remembered

82 Plain Legal Writing: Do It

> comes now
> further affiant sayeth not
> know all men by these presents
> said (adjective)
> same (noun)
> therefor
> to wit
> undersigned
> whereas
> wherefore, premises considered

None of those words and phrases should ever appear in a plain-English document.

If you encounter a word that's not listed here, how do you know if it's archaic? You can trust your common sense, or you can look up the word in a dictionary, legal dictionary, or legal-usage dictionary. For guidance on all things related to legal words, I recommend these sources:

- Bryan A. Garner, *Garner's Dictionary of Legal Usage* (3d ed. 2011)
- David Mellinkoff, *Mellinkoff's Dictionary of American Legal Usage* (2009)

Legalese and jargon

Train yourself to spot and revise words and phrases that only lawyers use. Consider them insider language, inapt for nonlawyers. A comprehensive list of legal words and insider jargon could fill this chapter, but here's a short list to get you started:

> action
> agent
> case at bar
> consideration
> duly
> execute (for sign)
> fee simple
> holding

instant case
intestate
pursuant to
shall

One simple test for legalese and jargon is to ask yourself whether a nonlawyer would give the word the same meaning you do. Take *action*, for example. To you, it's a lawsuit. To a nonlawyer, it's the process of doing—*taking action*. So when you write that clients can "bring an action against" someone, you're using legalese. Instead, write that they can "sue" someone. *Sue* may be a legal term, but it's one everyone knows. We're not striving to eliminate all legal words, just the ones only lawyers use.

Here's our representation contract again with the legalese highlighted.

Before—with legalese

Player **shall** reimburse Contract Advisor for all reasonable and necessary travel expenses actually incurred by Contract Advisor during the term of this agreement in the negotiation of Player's contract, but only if **such** expenses and approximate amounts of those expenses **shall** be approved in advance by Player.

The revision replaces *shall* per the recommendations in Chapter 4. It also replaces *such*, which is no more precise than *the*.

After—with everyday English

Player **agrees to** reimburse Contract Advisor for all reasonable and necessary travel expenses actually incurred by Contract Advisor during the term of this agreement in the negotiation of Player's contract, but only if **the** expenses and approximate amounts of those expenses **are** approved in advance by Player.

Terms of art

The law has terms of art. No one disputes this. Where plain-English advocates and typical lawyers disagree is on the number of terms of art. Some lawyers see them everywhere. But those who have studied the question, as Joseph Kimble has, assert that real terms of art are rare in the law: "True terms of art, technical terms with a fairly precise meaning, are far less common than lawyers tend to think."[2]

For example, many lawyers assume that when a court has issued an opinion construing or defining a term, it becomes a term of art. But a court decision construing or defining a word doesn't always make that word a term of art: case law containing the definitions is constantly evolving. As David Mellinkoff said 25 years ago: "You can't rely on precedent alone to make a term of art. ... There is too much of it. And it keeps changing."[3] So be sparing in labeling a word a term of art.

Even if you have a legitimate term of art, if you can cut it, cut it. Don't use a complex legal word in your document and simply fall back on the excuse that it is a term of art. Look it up. Consult a legal dictionary, a legal-usage dictionary, or *Words and Phrases*.[4] Ask someone. Be sure you need it and can't change it.

Yet sometimes a term of art is unavoidable. I once redrafted a notice about interest-rate changes for a credit-card agreement. I changed the phrase "our then-current rate" to "the interest rate we're using when you apply." An industry lawyer who was reviewing the draft suggested we retain "current" because in the industry it meant "within 30 days." Fine.

Another option is to use the term of art and then give a short, everyday-English explanation. Here's an example from our representation contract:

Before
> In performing these services, Contract Advisor acknowledges that he or she is acting in a **fiduciary capacity** on behalf of Player and agrees to act in such manner as to protect the best interests of

---

[2] Joseph Kimble, *Lifting the Fog of Legalese* 113 (2006).
[3] David Mellinkoff, *Legal Writing: Sense and Nonsense* 8 (1982).
[4] West's multi-volume collection of judicial definitions of words and phrases.

Player and assure effective representation of Player in individual contract negotiations ...

After

In performing these services, Contract Advisor acknowledges that he or she is acting in a **fiduciary capacity—meaning with the utmost good faith**—on behalf of Player and agrees to act in such manner as to protect the best interests of Player and assure effective representation of Player in individual contract negotiations ...

Here's another example of an indispensable term of art, *privilege*, found in a jury instruction:

You are instructed that you may not draw an adverse inference from the witness's claim of privilege.

I was the drafting consultant on the task force charged with redrafting this instruction. We all agreed that *privilege* was a legal term of art and that we ought to keep it. It has a relatively well-settled meaning in the law. But we also agreed that most nonlawyers would not know what it meant. So we retained the word *privilege* but defined it for the nonlegal reader:

A privilege is the right not to testify. You are instructed that you may not draw an adverse inference from the witness's claim of privilege.

I have more to say about this jury instruction in the next section.

Hyperformality

A natural, lawyerly impulse to sound serious and educated—or what I call *hyperformality*—drives a lot of dense legal writing. But hyperformality also arises from using outdated forms and from the misguided desire to intimidate or baffle the nonlegal reader. Shed that attitude; strive to communicate, not to impress.

Hyperformality causes lawyers to use all the problematic kinds of words we've just discussed: Latin and French, archaic words, insider legal jargon, and unnecessary terms of art. But these are only a small part of any legal text. What about all the other words? Even there, we can do more.

I want you to consider eliminating—here I go, opening myself up to savage criticism—"big words." Before I launch into a diatribe against big words, I want to remind you that it's not my goal to dumb down your vocabulary. It's not my goal to force all legal writing to a fourth-grade level. Rather, I'm focused on communicating legal concepts to nonlawyers. To do that, and to do it effectively, we need to bring our writing to their level.

I could give you a list of big words with their everyday-English equivalents, but someone else has already done that. Professor Joseph Kimble, the legal-writing expert, has published two articles that contain lists of big words and phrases with a parallel list of everyday English:

- Joseph Kimble, *Plain Words (Part 1)*, 80 *Mich. B.J.* 72 (Aug. 2001).
- Joseph Kimble, *Plain Words (Part 2)*, 80 *Mich. B.J.* 72 (Sept. 2001).

Go look at his lists (they're available free online) and get all the venting about dumbing down out of your system. After seeing his lists, I'm sure you'll agree I'm rather tame in my goals compared to Professor Kimble. Done?

Now you can put the lists aside. I want you to use your intuition. Immerse yourself in the world of plain English and put yourself inside the heads of your nonlegal readers. Figure out what words they're likely to know. Think about a time you did some reading in another field. When you're reading something unfamiliar, the simpler the words, the better, right?

We can all get inside the heads of our nonlegal readers. Here's a story offering evidence that nearly all lawyers, when they're motivated, are well aware of the kinds of words that ordinary readers won't understand.

In my work as the drafting consultant for a task force revising part of the Texas pattern jury charges into plain English, I attended a meeting of the jury-charges oversight committee; the committee's job was to read and approve changes to the jury charges. There were about 12 members of the oversight committee present, mainly lawyers and judges from around the state.

At one point, we were discussing a jury charge our task force had not yet revised. It was the charge quoted earlier, telling the jury what to do when a witness exercises a privilege:

> You are instructed that you may not draw an adverse inference from the witness's claim of privilege.

When this language was read out loud and was put on the projection screen, there was an immediate consensus—in fact, there was unanimity—that nonlawyers would not understand certain words in the instruction.

What particular words in this charge (besides *privilege*) do you think the members of the oversight committee realized would be hard for ordinary jurors? It's obvious, isn't it? The words were "draw an adverse inference." No one had to look it up. No one had to consult a usage dictionary. No one had to conduct a poll of nonlegal readers. All of us knew, instinctively, that these words were fancy, formal, and legal.

Specifically, *draw* as used in this phrase means "to conclude" and not "to sketch." As we've seen, it's fairly common for an everyday-English word to have an unconventional meaning when used by a lawyer. Next, *adverse* is just a fancy way of saying *bad*. And *inference* is problematic, too. Even lawyers get confused about *infer* and its forms.

You can recognize problematic words, just as we could. You simply have to tune your ear and mind to the level of the ordinary reader. By the way, once we decided that jurors should not draw even positive inferences from the witness's claim of privilege, we proposed this revision:

> A privilege is the right not to testify. Do not assume anything—good or bad—when a witness uses a privilege.

Crisp, natural, and personal

For legal documents that nonlawyers must read and understand, you want the text to be crisp. You want it to be natural—what I sometimes call "alive." And if possible, you want it to be personal. That way, readers feel that the document is speaking to them—not at them. One great technique for making your writing crisp, natural, and personal is shortening your average sentence length. You can also reduce complex prepositions, nominalizations, and passive voice. All these topics are discussed in Chapter 9.

But in my experience revising traditional legal language into plain English, the single most effective technique for making a document crisp, natural, and personal is to use the personal pronouns *you, I, we,* and *us.*

This isn't a new idea. Language expert Rudolf Flesch recommended this technique in the 1970s. He considered what he called "the *you* style" to be indispensable for plain English.[5]

Two examples can help make the point.

Imagine that your parent has died and you've been named the administrator or personal representative of the estate. You've decided to hire a lawyer to help you handle the matter. The lawyer hands you an "hourly fee agreement" that contains the following language (oh—and pretend you're not a lawyer):

> Attorney is about to undertake the performance of substantial legal services on behalf of the Personal Representative, for which Attorney shall be paid fees and costs. The Personal Representative has retained Attorney to provide legal services to the Personal Representative for administration of the probate estate.

I hope you'll agree that this text has several problems. But we can improve it tremendously, and make it seem more immediate to the reader, if we simply use the words *you* and *me*:

---

5. Rudolf Flesch, *How to Write Plain English: A Book for Lawyers and Consumers* 44 (1979).

Plain-English Words 89

I am about to undertake the performance of substantial legal services on behalf of you [your behalf], for which I shall be paid fees and costs. You have retained me to provide legal services to you for administration of the probate estate.

Some might object that the words *attorney* and *personal representative* were defined elsewhere, and consistency requires us to use them throughout. But couldn't we define *you* and *I* to mean personal representative and attorney and use them throughout.

Here's another example of the *you* approach that adds *we* for the entity that drafted the text. It highlights two other benefits: when you use awkward initials and when you insist on working around personal pronouns, you sound like a machine. You can avoid both those practices with the *you/we* approach.

Original

Therapeutic Recovery Care Hospital for Children ("TRCHC") has provided this web site for educational and informational purposes only. The material contained herein is believed to be complete and generally in accord with accepted standards at the time of publication. However, because of the possibility of human error and changes in medical science, TRCHC and its employees do not warrant that the information contained herein is in every respect accurate or complete, and thus, are not responsible for any errors or omissions or for the results obtained from the use of such information. TRCHC makes no representation or warranties, expressed or implied, and disclaims any liability for injury and any other damages which result from an individual using techniques discussed on this site.

The stiff and impersonal tone and hard-to-pronounce initials arise from avoiding personal pronouns. And you can spot some archaic words and some hyperformality, right? Let's fix it all:

Original	**Revision**
Therapeutic Recovery Care Hospital for Children ("TRCHC") has	We (the Therapeutic Recovery Care Hospital for Children and

provided this web site for educational and informational purposes only.	its employees) provide this website for education and information only.
The material contained herein is believed to be complete and generally in accord with accepted standards at the time of publication.	We believe the material here is complete and that it generally met accepted standards when we published it.
However, because of the possibility of human error and changes in medical science, TRCHC and its employees do not warrant that the information contained herein is in every respect accurate or complete, and thus, are not responsible for any errors or omissions or for the results obtained from the use of such information.	But because people make mistakes and medical science changes, we don't warrant that the information is entirely accurate or complete. We aren't responsible for any errors or omissions or for the results if you use this information.
TRCHC makes no representation or warranties, expressed or implied, and disclaims any liability for injury or any other damages which result from an individual using techniques discussed on this site.	We make no representations or warranties, expressed or implied, and we're not liable for injury or any other damages if you use techniques discussed on this site.

I can boil this chapter down to this: think of your reader. If you do, you'll banish foreign and archaic words. You'll never write for nonlawyers as if they were legal insiders. And you'll speak directly to your reader with *you* and with everyday words whenever you can.

Plain-English Sentences

> In plain-English legal drafting, manage your average sentence length and beware of overlong sentences. Put actors in your sentences when you can. Punctuate for precision. And cut, cut, cut.

When you're drafting legal text for a nonlegal audience, what's the longest any single sentence should be? And what's a good average sentence length? Countless legal writing experts have discussed these questions, and many have offered recommendations. Let me tell you what I think.

Let's begin with sentence length. Why do legal sentences often end up so long? Perhaps it's because of the cases we read in law school. Long sentences abound in judicial opinions. In fact, that influence is so strong on students that many years ago I began to track the longest sentences in student papers. For a number of years, the record for the longest sentence was 97 words. But just a few years ago that record was shattered by a student-written sentence of 114 words. Of course, that's an aberration. But it perhaps hints at the overall problem lawyers have with long sentences.

Perhaps we write long sentences, particularly in transactional documents, because we believe in what Howard Darmstadter calls a myth—that an idea and all its qualifications must be contained in a single sentence:

> When a general statement is subject to an exception or two, why do drafters feel that the exceptions must be packed into the same sentence as the general statement? For many drafters, the unit of truth is the sentence.... [E]ach sentence must be true taken by itself—that is, its truth or falsity cannot be allowed to depend on some other sentence or sentences.... Such a position is, of course, ridiculous.[1]

In their excellent book, *Clear Understandings*, Ronald Goldfarb and James Raymond debunk the single-sentence myth as well:

> [Lawyers] think that in order to achieve clear understandings, they must stuff every related idea into a single sentence between an initial capital letter and a final period. They are, of course, wrong.[2]

So use multiple sentences. And watch your maximum sentence length.

Maximum sentence length

Any single sentence longer than 45 words will probably challenge a nonlawyer. In fact, depending on the complexity of the sentence structure and the density of the subject matter, even a much shorter sentence can be a challenge. The goal is not to challenge the reader but to inform and communicate.

Of course, if the sentence is well constructed, especially if it contains elegant, parallel phrases in a series, it can be even longer than 45 words and still be understandable. So my recommendation of 45 words as a maximum sentence length is just that, a recommendation.

If you agree with me that you must watch your maximum sentence length, be practical about it. You don't count the number of words in your sentences as you write. Rather, controlling sentence length occurs primarily during the edit. So if, on reading a single

---

1. Howard Darmstadter, *Hereof, Thereof, and Everywhereof: A Contrarian Guide to Legal Drafting* 41 (2002).
2. Ronald L. Goldfarb & James C. Raymond, *Clear Understandings: A Guide to Legal Writing* 47 (1982).

sentence, I find myself growing weary or bogged down, I select the sentence, check the word count, and assess the length. If the length is more than 45 words, I revise.

Average sentence length

When I ask lawyers about average sentence length in a public setting, such as one of my seminars, I get a variety of answers. For example, I've had a lawyer suggest that 35 words per sentence is a good average. That's too long, I think. But I've also had a lawyer suggest that eight words per sentence is a good average. That's not realistic, I think. Generally speaking, in a legal text aimed at nonlegal readers, and excluding citations, the average sentence length should be 20 words per sentence or fewer.

But you don't have to take my word for it. Here are recommended average sentence lengths from the experts:

- Below 25, says Richard Wydick in *Plain English for Lawyers*.
- About 22, say Anne Enquist and Laurel Currie Oates in *Just Writing: Grammar, Punctuation, and Style for the Legal Writer*.
- About 20, says Bryan A. Garner in *Legal Writing in Plain English*.

And when you write about complex subjects, push the average length down. In *Writing to Win*, litigator and teacher Steven Stark says that the more complicated your information is, the shorter your sentences should be.[3]

By the way, Microsoft Word can tell you your average sentence length for any selected text. Go to your Word preferences options and in the Proofing or Spelling and Grammar section, check the box that says "Show readability statistics." You may also need to check the box that says "Check grammar with spelling" to get the readability-statistics function to work. This is too bad, because the grammar checker isn't very good; I estimate that at least half the

---

3. Steven D. Stark, *Writing to Win: The Legal Writer* 33 (1999).

things it suggests are just plain wrong. A solution is to go into Settings and uncheck all the grammar boxes. The program is still "checking" your grammar, but has nothing to check for. Now, each time you finish a spell-check, you'll see a display telling you your average sentence length. Note that if the text has citations, headings, and tabulated lists, these will drive the average sentence length down. You can get a more realistic sense of your average sentence length by selecting and checking shorter sections that don't include citations, headings, or tabulated lists.

Be practical about average sentence length and try not to become obsessed. If your average sentence length is in the teens, that's great. If it's higher than 20, you might search for and revise the longest sentences. And when I suggest an average sentence length, I don't imply that all sentences should be of that length. Rather, you should vary your sentence length appropriately to avoid a choppy writing style.

Beyond sentence length, you can do a number of things to write readable sentences.

Replace nominalizations

A "nominalization" is a verb that has been turned into a noun. When I say "make a payment" in place of "pay," I am using a nominalization. Nominalizations abound in legal writing:

Nominalized form	Verb form
your attendance is required	you must attend
bring suit against	sue
make an application	apply
interpose an objection	object
have knowledge of	know
reach an agreement	agree

When you use a nominalization, you must add extra words to get the same meaning. When you use a lot of nominalizations, you need a lot of extra words, and you usually end up putting your reader to sleep.

Nominalizations are a classic hallmark of traditional legalese. So one way to control your sentence length, avoid legalese, and make your sentences speak to the reader is to replace nominalizations.

In this excerpt from a law-firm website disclaimer, the nominalizations are highlighted:

With nominalizations

> **Reproduction** of all or part of the contents of this page in any form is prohibited other than for individual use and it may not be recopied and shared with a third party. The **permission** to recopy by an individual does not allow for **incorporation** of this material or any part of it in any work or publication, whether in hard copy, electronic, or any other form.

With verbs instead

> You may not **reproduce** all or part of the contents of this page in any form—other than for individual use, and you may not recopy and share it with a third party. If we **permit** you to recopy, you may not **incorporate** this material or any part of it into any work or publication, whether in hard copy, electronic, or any other form.

The revised text is only four words shorter, but it's more alive. In other words, it's beginning to speak to the reader, instead of droning on in dull legalese. So when you edit, look for nouns, especially big nouns, that could be verbs. (One hint is that many nominalizations end in "-ion.") Then replace the nouns with the verb form.

Practice consistent parallelism

Express related ideas in parallel form. This is fairly easy to say, but the trick is to do it consistently, without fail. Your reward will be text that is easy to read and understand. In fact, to the extent you write in perfectly parallel form, you have freedom to create longer sentences. Even long sentences, when constructed with a lead-in and a series of perfectly parallel phrases, can be easy to read.

Drafting for the nonlegal audience presents many opportunities for parallelism. Strict standards for parallelism require that all the items or phrases in the series can fit directly with the lead-in and that all the items or phrases in the series begin with the same part of speech. To test for parallelism, tabulate the items or phrases in the series (put each on its own line), even if you won't tabulate them in the final document. For example:

Original—not parallel

> Publisher has the right to determine (1) the number of copies to be printed, (2) the method and style of the print and binding, (3) how to advertise and sell the book, (4) publish the book in one or more volumes and in any style it thinks is best suited to its sale, and (5) set the price of the book.

The easiest way to see that the original is not parallel is to tabulate it—that is, to place each numbered item on its own line:

Nonparallel original—as tabulated

> Publisher has the right to determine
> 1. the number of copies to be printed,
> 2. the method and style of the print and binding,
> 3. how to advertise and sell the book,
> 4. publish the book in one or more volumes and in any style it thinks is best suited to its sale, and
> 5. set the price of the book.

Now we can see that the individual items don't all fit with the lead-in "determine." What's more, the numbered items don't begin with the same part of speech. How does this happen? Generally, when the phrases in a series are presented in a paragraph format rather than a tabulated format, the writer can sometimes lose track of the lead-in. And the longer the list of phrases, the more likely it is that the drafter will forget how each phrase is to begin.

For ease of reading, be scrupulous in applying strict parallelism.

Parallel revision

Publisher has the right
1. to determine the number of copies to be printed,
2. to determine the method and style of the print and binding,
3. to determine how to advertise and sell the book,
4. to publish the book in one or more volumes and in any style it thinks is best suited to its sale, and
5. to set the price of the book.

Note: In applying strict parallelism, you need not repeat the preposition *to* in each item. You could change the lead-in to "Publisher has the right to" and then begin each item with a verb. Your choice.

Find "actors" for your sentences and put them to work

Plain-English legal drafting requires you to constantly consider this question: Who is doing the action in this sentence—who is the "actor"? By finding actors for your sentences, you'll make the text more immediate, alive, and readable. And you'll avoid some common pitfalls.

To fully discuss the use of actors in our sentences, we must understand the passive voice. A passive-voice construction exists when you use a form of the verb *be* (*be, am, is, are, was, were, being, been*) followed by a past participle (the form of a verb that could fit here: *have* _____, as in *have walked* and *have written*). Thus, the following are passive voice constructions:

If the market price is increased to $8,000 ...
After the notices are received ...
The full purchase price shall be paid ...

Each contains a form of the verb *be* and a past participle:

is + increased

98 Plain Legal Writing: Do It

    are + received
    be + paid

Please also notice that there is no actor in any of these examples. This is the primary drawback of the passive voice in plain-English drafting: the absence of an actor. The key to revising passive voice constructions is to identify the appropriate actor—acknowledging that in some circumstances it may be okay to leave the actor unidentified. In the following sentence, for example, the absence of an actor is entirely appropriate:

    If the market price is increased to $8,000, ...

In this sentence, who is the actor? In other words, who is it that is increasing the purchase price? In fact, it is no one. There are some circumstances in drafting in which an action simply occurs and it is entirely appropriate to state it without identifying an actor. Still, we could improve this text by eliminating the passive voice and converting to present tense, active voice:

    If the market price increases to $8,000, ...

But most of the time, we would do well to identify an actor as we eliminate the passive voice:

    After we receive the notices ...
    You agree to pay the full purchase price ...

These conversions to the active voice have a number of advantages. The sentences are shorter. The tone is direct and vigorous. The subject matter of the sentence is concrete and clear. And we've imposed a contractual obligation directly on an actor rather than left it floating—as if the obligation would somehow just happen.

Inappropriate passive-voice constructions abound in traditional legal drafting. Here are three real-world examples that struck me as particularly problematic because in each case, the passive-voice construction fails to impose a contractual obligation on a party:

All payments due before April 30, 2005, shall continue to be sent to the lender at the address set forth above. [Sent by whom?]

Insurance coverage amounts or types must be revised to fully cover the property. [Who must revise them?]

Permits are to be secured before construction of the residential pool can commence. [Who must secure the permits?]

Whenever it's possible to eliminate the passive voice and impose an obligation directly on one of the parties, you should do it.

Wordiness

When you can cut words and not lose meaning, do it. Shorter is better, as long as you don't lose content. Granted, a plain-English version of a text sometimes ends up longer than the original, especially if you've inserted explanations of legal terms. Still, whenever you can, you should cut, cut, cut.

Things to look for:

nominalizations	using the verb form usually eliminates words
modifiers	duly, applicable, expressly, further (saying it directly is usually better)
general redundancies	at this point in time (now), during such time as (when)
legal redundancies	cease and desist, above and foregoing, true and correct
redundant lists	sell, convey, and transfer; ordered, adjudged, and decreed
legalisms	prior to (before), pursuant to (under), subsequent to (after), in the event that (if)

Here's an example of wordiness from some pattern jury instructions:

Original

Do not make personal inspections, observations, investigations, or experiments nor personally view premises, things, or articles not produced in court.

Some suggested revisions:

Original	Suggestions
Do not make personal inspections	Change the nominalization: *make personal inspections* becomes *inspect*
inspections, observations, investigations, or experiments	Consolidate the list by eliminating true redundancies or by using broader terms: Is *inspecting* truly different in this context from *observing*?
nor personally view premises	Cut unnecessary modifiers: Is there a difference between *personally viewing* and *viewing*?
things or articles not produced in court	Cut redundancies: Is there a difference between *things* and *articles*?

Revision

Do not view or inspect places or things from this case unless they are presented as evidence in court.

Punctuation

This isn't a comprehensive guide to punctuation. It's just a review of some important highlights for plain legal drafting.

Serial commas

Rather than discuss all the rules for commas, I'd like to focus on one important comma in legal drafting: the serial comma.

For legal documents, always include a comma after the coordinating conjunction in a series of three or more items. Granted, this is a formal approach to writing; for informal writing, such as journalism and literature, the serial comma is often omitted. Still, even though you're writing legal documents for a nonlegal audience, you should adopt the more formal rule of always using the serial comma. The reason is simple, according to Bryan Garner: omitting it can cause ambiguities, but including it never will.[4] In all the following examples, the serial comma is used correctly:

> Do not view premises, things, or articles not produced in court.
>
> The statement shall set forth the fees charged to the player for individual salary negotiations, management of players' assets, and any other miscellaneous services.
>
> All claims, whether for money damages, penalties, or equitable relief, shall be resolved by binding arbitration.

Many lawyers, particularly transactional drafters, resist using the serial comma. But because it eliminates confusion about whether the final two items in the series are one unit or two, its use is preferred. What's more, its absence has caused litigation. I received the sentence below from a lawyer seeking to hire me as an expert witness. The text has other problems, but please notice that the last two items in this lengthy series are not separated by a comma (highlighted):

> "Cash" means cash, cash equivalents, other short term investments having a readily ascertainable market value, investments held in board designated funds, excluding, however, any such assets whose use is limited to payment of current liabilities, **all Trustee held funds and malpractice funds** ...

The parties to this litigation were, in part, disputing whether "Trustee held funds" and "malpractice funds" were one thing or two

---

4. Bryan A. Garner, *Garner's Dictionary of Legal Usage* 731 (3d ed. 2011).

things. I believe a transactional drafter, following a widespread but faulty convention, omitted the comma between the last two items. The revision would look like this:

> "Cash" means cash, cash equivalents, other short term investments having a readily ascertainable market value, investments held in board designated funds, excluding, however, any such assets whose use is limited to payment of current liabilities, **all Trustee held funds, and malpractice funds** ...

If an appeal to authority will convince you, here it is:

- Put commas between all items in a series.[5]
- Always put a comma before the *and* or *or* in a series.[6]
- Use commas between items in a series.[7]
- Use commas to separate the items in a series.[8]
- Always use the serial comma.[9]

Semicolons

In legal drafting, the semicolon has primarily two uses:

1. it separates the items in a numbered list; and
2. it separates items in a series when one or more of the items has its own internal commas.

The two numbered items above show the first use. Even if the items in the series could be separated by commas, in legal drafting, the convention is to use the semicolon if you've numbered the items.

The second primary use of the semicolon prevents confusion about which are the main items in a series and which are subordinate or internal items embedded within the main items. Look at the following two examples and note that the fourth item in the

---

5. Terri LeClercq, *Expert Legal Writing* 152 (1995).
6. Robert J. Martineau & Michael B. Salerno, *Legal, Legislative, and Rule Drafting in Plain English* 68 (2005).
7. Anne Enquist & Laurel Currie Oates, *Just Writing: Grammar, Punctuation, and Style for the Legal Writer* 244 (2d ed. 2005).
8. Richard C. Wydick, *Plain English for Lawyers* 88 (5th ed. 2005).
9. Bryan A. Garner, *The Elements of Legal Style* 15 (2d ed. 2002).

main series, beginning with *investments*, contains internal commas. The original, which I mentioned above, caused litigation that might have been avoided if it had been punctuated as in the revised example.

Original

"Cash" means cash, cash equivalents, other short term investments having a readily ascertainable market value, investments held in board designated funds, excluding, however, any such assets whose use is limited to payment of current liabilities, all Trustee held funds and malpractice funds.

Revised

"Cash" means cash; cash equivalents; other short-term investments having a readily ascertainable market value; investments held in board-designated funds, excluding, however, any such assets whose use is limited to payment of current liabilities; all Trustee-held funds; and malpractice funds.

I grant you that the text is now a little heavy on punctuation. But that's far better than the confusion and ambiguity that resulted from the use of commas alone.

Colons

In legal drafting, the colon primarily introduces lists. The standard and traditional convention is that the text before a colon should be an independent clause. That is, it should be a complete sentence, capable of standing on its own. But modern English and the conventions of legal drafting have changed this rule. Generally, it is acceptable to use a colon after almost anything, even a dependent clause or phrase.

As a practical matter, what this means is that more formal-sounding, lead-in sentences can be replaced with shorter phrases:

Correct but formal

"Cash" means all of the following:
    a.   cash;

b. cash equivalents;
   c. other short-term investments having a readily ascertainable market value; and
   d. investments held in board-designated funds …

Also correct, but informal

"Cash" means:
   a. cash;
   b. cash equivalents;
   c. other short-term investments having a readily ascertainable market value; and
   d. investments held in board-designated funds …

Dashes

The em dash, or just the "dash," is an entirely appropriate punctuation mark to use in legal drafting. It's particularly useful to emphasize parenthetical information when using parentheses would have a tendency to deemphasize the information. The em dash—like those in this sentence—is the longest of the three horizontal punctuation marks, the others being the hyphen (-), used to divide words and connect compound modifiers, and the en dash (–), used for number spans.

You can also insert and example into a sentence with a pair of em dashes, and the examples will then take on emphasis. This advice comes from Professor Paul Marx in his excellent book, *The Modern Rules of Style*,[10] and this example comes from a ticket I purchased:

Original

Holder consents to the search of all bags, packages, or any other container brought to the Museum or its premises.

---

10. Paul Marx, *The Modern Rules of Style* 50 (2007).

Revision

> You consent to the search of all personal items—bags, packages, or any other container—brought to the Museum or its premises.

Pay attention to your sentences, to their length and complexity. Pay attention to actors and use more of them. Pay attention to punctuation. These things matter, and your attention to them will pay off in clearer writing.

Testing Your Plain-English Drafts

> Test your plain-English drafts with several testing techniques, both formal and informal. Seek and accept critiques and feedback on the plain-English text you produce.

Once you've completed your plain legal document, you should test it on the intended audience—nonlawyers. No matter how carefully you write, and no matter what readability scales you use (see Chapter 10), there's no substitute for feedback from readers. Sophisticated testing is not always feasible, and you may not always have a lot of time. But whenever possible, do at least some testing.

Benefits of testing

Most writers aren't comfortable with critique. It's difficult to accept comments and criticism. It's difficult to acknowledge that what seems clear to us is a muddle to someone else. But in my experience, testing always improves the text.

Testing helps you uncover mistakes. As embarrassing as it is to have testers tell you that you misspelled a word or left out a comma, it is far less embarrassing than having the mistake survive into the final document.

Testing allows you to get a true gauge of the audience's preferences. Most of the time, when preparing a plain legal document, you're making assumptions about what the reader needs, how the reader will use the document, and what the reader already knows.

108 Plain Legal Writing: Do It

When you test your document on the intended audience, you get facts.

For example, when I participated on a task force that revised pattern jury charges, I remember watching live mock-jury deliberations and realizing that the jurors were misunderstanding the word *unanimous* in the context of certain instructions. Some questions the jury had to answer could be agreed upon by 10 of the 12 jurors, but for other questions, agreement on the answer had to be unanimous. In fact, the answering of some later questions was conditioned on unanimous answers to a previous question. The language was phrased like this: "If the jury was unanimous in answering Question 5, proceed to answer Question 6."

I could see and hear the jurors discussing whether *unanimous* in that instruction meant all 12 jurors or just the same 10 jurors who had agreed on an earlier answer. The jurors mistakenly believed that if the same 10 people agreed on question 6 as had agreed on question 5, that was unanimous. Having learned of this confusion, the task force revised the draft instructions: "If all 12 of you agreed on Question 5, then answer Question 6."

Testing also produces empirical evidence to support the effectiveness of plain English. For example, it might have been difficult to persuade a pattern-jury-charges oversight committee that typical jurors misunderstood the word *unanimous*. But because there was testing, the task force had videotaped evidence. And we had videotapes showing jurors deliberating with our new instructions, which excluded the word *unanimous*. With the new instructions, there was no confusion.

Testing methods

Here I'll describe some plain-English testing methods I've used. For further information on testing, consult these sources:

- Michele M. Asprey, *Plain Language for Lawyers*, ch. 17 (4th ed. 2010)
- Christine Mowat, *A Plain Language Handbook for Legal Writers*, ch. 5 (1998)

Informal testing

Sometimes you can just ask someone about a piece of writing on the spot, orally. "Here. Read this. What do you think?" The more specific the question, the more it may come off like an interrogation, but the better the feedback is likely to be. You can move from broad (what do you think?) to moderately specific (do you understand this paragraph?) to narrowly specific (what does this sentence or word mean?).

One of my favorite testing techniques is to send an email message to a group of my friends and solicit their input on a piece of legal writing. Usually, since it's in writing, I'm able to ask narrower questions and get better feedback.

An easy approach is to send before-and-after versions (not labeled) and ask which they prefer. I've also sent a piece of text and asked recipients to explain what it means in their own words. And I've asked recipients to read a piece of text and answer multiple-choice questions about it. In reality you're giving them a test, but if you tell them it's to improve legal writing, they'll usually be glad to help.

Another informal way to test a piece of plain legal writing is to ask a nonlawyer to read and critique it. I've used this technique effectively on a few occasions.

Sometimes you must persuade readers that you sincerely want their candid reactions. Often, those without legal training assume that if they don't understand something or if the writing seems dense, it's because they aren't lawyers. Usually, if you explain your goals and genuinely accept their feedback, you'll be able to persuade them that the reactions of a typical nonlawyer are precisely what you're looking for.

Here are two examples of the kind of informal testing I've done.

Example 1—Baseball ticket

I once sent the following language to 10 friends, none of whom was a lawyer; most were college-educated; one had completed only high school, and one had a Ph.D. I asked them to pay specific attention to the boldface words.

The holder is admitted on condition, and by use of this ticket agrees, that he will not transmit or aid in transmitting any description, account, picture or reproduction of the baseball game or exhibition to which this ticket admits him. Breach of the foregoing will automatically terminate this **license**.

The holder assumes all risk and dangers incidental to the game of baseball including specifically (but not exclusively) the danger of being injured by thrown or batted balls and agrees that the participating clubs, their **agents** and players are not liable for injuries resulting from such causes. The management reserves the right to revoke the license granted by this ticket.

I then asked them to answer these two questions:
1. What does the word *license* mean here?
   a. a permit from an authority to do or own a thing (like a driver's license)
   b. permission to enter property that would otherwise be a trespass
   c. don't know
2. Who are the *agents* mentioned?
   a. employees who work for the clubs
   b. sports agents representing the players
   c. don't know

On question 1, six correctly answered b, three answered a, and one answered c. On question 2, six correctly answered a, and four answered b. Those answers reflect moderate confusion. Thus, in revising the language, I did not use the legal words *license* or *agents*.

Baseball ticket revised

This ticket admits you to the event listed on the front. By using it, you agree not to broadcast or help broadcast any descriptions or pictures of the event. If you do, you must leave the event.

Test Your Plain-English Drafts 111

By using this ticket, you accept the risks of attending a baseball game. For example, you could be hit by thrown or batted balls or injured in other ways. Stadium management, its representatives, the teams, and the players are not responsible for those injuries.

Management can revoke this ticket and remove you from the event.

Example 2—Statement on alternative dispute resolution

In revising a bit of statutorily mandated language, I decided to avoid the phrases *nonjudicial settlement* and *alternative dispute resolution*, believing them to be complex, insider language for lawyers. Here's the original language:

> I am aware that it is the policy of the state to promote the amicable and **nonjudicial settlement** of disputes involving children and families. I am aware of **alternative dispute resolution** methods, including mediation. While I recognize that **alternative dispute resolution** is an alternative to and not a substitute for a trial and that this case may be tried if it is not settled, I represent to the court that I will attempt in good faith to resolve before final trial contested issues in this case by **alternative dispute resolution** without the necessity of court intervention.

Instead, I used the phrases *out-of-court settlement* and *non-court solutions*:

> By signing this statement, you affirm that:
> - You know that the state promotes peaceful, **out-of-court settlements** of family-law cases.
> - You know about **non-court solutions**, including mediation.
> - You know that **non-court solutions** are an option and not a substitute for a trial.
> - You know that this case may go to court if it is not settled.
> - You promise to try—in good faith—to resolve this case out of court.

I asked a lawyer to read the revision and make suggestions, and one suggestion was that "*out-of-court settlement* is redundant. All settlements are out of court." I wondered if nonlawyers thought so, and so I asked. Here's the question I sent my 10 friends:

1. If a lawsuit is "settled out of court" or there is an "out-of-court settlement," what does that mean?
    a. The people and lawyers in the lawsuit resolved it without the judge.
    b. The people and lawyers in the lawsuit resolved it with the judge's help.
    c. Either a or b.

Eight answered c, and two answered a. Thus, it seems that most nonlawyers think of settlement as possibly involving the judge or occurring in court.

Informal testing does have drawbacks. Because it's informal, your results may not be statistically valid. So informal testing generally produces only anecdotal support rather than solid evidence. Yet this is often enough for making helpful edits and revisions.

Formal testing

You can use some of the same testing methods mentioned above in more formal settings. Generally, this means the test takers are not acquainted with you, are selected randomly, and are representative of the document's intended audience.

Once you have a group of test takers, you can ask them to read and compare before-and-after versions of the text. You should guide their comparisons with clear instructions and probably with specific questions. You can also ask one group of test takers to read the original and answer questions, and then ask another group to read the revision and answer the same questions. Compare the results.

I participated in a two-day test of pattern jury charges that was handled this way.[1] On day one, 48 mock jurors, divided into 4 groups of 12, deliberated on a mock lawsuit using the original pattern jury charges. On day two, 48 different mock jurors repeated the process using revised jury charges. Because the educational and demographic makeup of the two groups was similar, we validly compared the results of the tests. Incidentally, the revised jury instructions scored better than the original did.

For example, both sets of jurors answered a series of 10 rating questions like this:

The instructions were understandable.
Not at all   Very much
1   2   3   4   5   6

Both sets then answered a series of *true/false/don't know* questions like this:

The case presented before you is a civil action and not a criminal action.

(The case actually was a civil action, and 84 percent of the jurors using the original jury charges got the question right. But 100 percent of the jurors using the revised instructions got it right.)

One interesting thing we learned came from this question about the original jury charges:

To find that the Defendant committed [civil] fraud, the Plaintiff has to prove only that one of the four elements for fraud has been met.

The correct answer is *false* because the Plaintiff must prove all four elements. Yet only 20 percent of jurors using the original charges got the answer right. We had watched the jurors deliberate, and we were able to see what had caused confusion. The elements of fraud were presented like this:

---

1. The information in this section is taken from a nonpublic report: *State Bar of Texas Juror Comprehension Field Testing of Pattern Jury Charges* (2006).

Fraud occurs when—
a. A party makes a material misrepresentation,
b. The misrepresentation is made with knowledge of its falsity or made recklessly without any knowledge of the truth,
c. The misrepresentation is made with the intention that it should be acted upon, and
d. The other party relies on the misrepresentation and thereby suffers injury.

This list of elements uses the standard convention for tabulated lists in which you place a comma after each item and the conjunction (*and*) after the next-to-last item. We had assumed the jurors would know what lawyers know: this convention means all the elements must be proved. But as we watched the jurors deliberate, we could see and hear that they were unsure. The presence of the single *and* led some to believe not all the elements had to be proved—that it was a list from which any one could be proved to establish fraud or that only items 1, 3, and 4 had to be proved.

So we changed our revised jury charges to emphasize that all the elements had to be proved (bold italics show the key changes):

Fraud occurs when **all of these elements** are present—
a. a party makes a material misrepresentation, **and**
b. the party makes the misrepresentation knowing it is false or makes the representation recklessly without knowing if it is true or false, **and**
c. the party makes the misrepresentation and intends that the other party should act on it, and
d. the other party relies on the misrepresentation and suffers injury from relying on it.

When the second set of jurors used this revised instruction, 68 percent of them got the question right.

If you have the time and the patience, one of the best kinds of formal testing to use on a plain legal document is a read-and-apply test. Again, you use two groups of test takers. The first group reads the original legal text and then uses it to solve a problem, fill out a form, or answer a legal question. A second group completes the same exercises using the revised text. Professor Joseph Kimble has used this approach on groups of legal secretaries and law students with excellent results.[2]

Formal testing has drawbacks, too. Mainly, it's expensive. In our jury-charge testing, we hired a pricey jury consultant who in turn hired an actor to play the judge and paid a per diem to the mock jurors. These expenses added up. What's more, it's often time-consuming, and it can be difficult to create valid test questions.

But to genuinely improve your plain-English drafts, you must test. Even the most experienced experts at legal drafting recognize this. Candid feedback from the intended audience will improve the writing and expose problems you weren't aware of.

---

2. Joseph Kimble, *Answering the Critics of Plain Language*, 5 Scribes J. Legal Writing 51, 69–71 (1994–1995).

Using Readability Tests

To improve your plain-English drafting, learn the appropriate role for readability tests, then use them wisely.

Understanding readability scales

Readability scales are mechanical tests writers can use to get a sense of the readability of a piece of text. Probably the most well-known of the readability scales is the Flesch Readability Scale, now commonly called Flesch Reading Ease, created by Rudolf Flesch. Flesch created his readability scale while doing graduate work at Columbia University. His first readability scale was based on several factors, including "human" words (*I, you, we*) and vocabulary lists. He eventually simplified the test to rely only on average word length in syllables and average sentence length in words.[1]

There are other readability tests. The Dale-Chill formula was created in 1948 and updated in 1995. The Gunning Fog Index was created in 1952. The SMOG index (Simple Measure of Gobbledygook) was created in 1969.[2] But because Microsoft uses Flesch Reading Ease in its Microsoft Word software, it's the most frequently used and well known.

---

1. Rudolf Flesch, *How to Write Plain English: A Book for Lawyers and Consumers* (1979).
2. Mark Hochhauser, *What Readability Expert Witnesses Should Know*, 54 Clarity 38 (Nov. 2005).

Microsoft Word will calculate a Flesch Reading Ease score for any selected text. Go to your Word preferences options and in the Proofing or Spelling and Grammar section, check the box that says "Show readability statistics." You'll also need to check the box that says "Check grammar with spelling" to get the readability-statistics function to work. (Remember to go into Settings and uncheck any useless grammar items.) Now, each time you finish a spell-check, you'll see a display telling you your average sentence length, your Flesch Reading Ease score, and your Flesch–Kincaid grade level, along with other statistical information.

What this means for Flesch Reading Ease is that Microsoft Word is assessing your average sentence length and average word length and assigning a score. The Flesch Reading Ease scale runs from 0 to 100, and the higher the score, the more readable the text. So a score of 0 means the text is extremely difficult, and a score of 100 means it is extremely easy—a child's level. Flesch himself said a score of 60 constitutes "plain English." For my money, any legal document that can score 50 or higher is pretty good. Most legal writing scores in the 30s.

Besides the Flesch scale, plain-English drafters can also use something called the Flesch–Kincaid grade level. This formula, also available in Microsoft Word, applies a numerical grade level from 1 to about 20. The grade level corresponds to the number of years of post-kindergarten education a reader would need to comprehend the document. For example, most lawyers would prefer to read at grade level of 19: 12 years of primary education + 4 years of college + 3 years of law school.

The Flesch–Kincaid grade level isn't exact or perfect. It relies partly on vocabulary lists that students of a certain grade level should know, but some of the lists haven't been updated since the 1940s.[3] So you simply get a general sense of the readability of the text.

---

3. *Id.*

Using readability scales

Remember that Flesch relies on sentence length and word length, so the reading-ease calculation punishes long sentences and big words. Of course, serious writers know that even long sentences can be easy to understand if they're well-constructed. And of course, in legal drafting, sometimes big words are necessary. For these reasons, the Flesch scale is a limited tool.

That's why, on occasion, writing experts criticize the use of the Flesch scale, pointing out that it's a mindless word-and-syllable counter. It knows nothing about tone, style, or grammatical correctness. It can't help you write correctly or in a way that makes sense if you don't already know how.

Of course, they're right. Take this sentence:

Issued order the judge an.

It scores well on the Flesch scale even though it makes no sense. That's why readability scales are simply one tool to aid in plain-English legal drafting. They give you a sense of how understandable your text is, but they generally shouldn't be an end unto themselves.[4]

For example, some states require that certain consumer documents score at certain levels on the Flesch scale. In Texas, at least three different kinds of consumer contracts won't be approved by regulating boards unless they score 40 or higher on the Flesch scale.[5] Using a rigid numerical Flesch score may not be ideal, but it's better than letting lawyers prepare consumer documents with no regard for readability.

Rather than rely too heavily on any one readability assessment, I like to consider a number of factors when I seek to revise a piece of traditional legal writing into plain English.

First, I like to measure the before-and-after average sentence length. Long sentences are hard on readers, especially nonlawyers.

[4.] William H. DuBay, *Smart Language: Readers, Readability, and the Grading of Text* 113 (2007).
[5.] *See, e.g.*, Tex. Admin. Code § 3.602(b)(1).

We lawyers—having spent at least three years and often much longer reading statutes, judicial opinions, and documents prepared by lawyers—are used to long sentences. Nonlegal readers are not. Assessing your average sentence length is pretty easy to do and was explained in Chapter 9.

Second, I like to measure the before-and-after Flesch Reading Ease score. If I can move a document that originally scored in the 30s to a score above 50, I consider it a great improvement. I try not to get hung up on achieving a 60—Flesch's goal for plain English. Depending on the complexity of the subject matter, scoring 60 may be difficult or even impossible.

Third, I like to measure the before-and-after Flesch–Kincaid grade level. For complicated legal materials, I often aim for a grade level of about 10. My thinking is that if a 10th grader could understand what I'm writing, I'm doing a pretty good job. But I've taken complicated legal texts and converted them into simpler texts that have scored at a 7th- or 8th-grade level.

Here's a story that illustrates the appropriate use of readability scores and other factors in assessing the readability of a document.

I was once hired by a bank to rewrite a series of home-loan documents into plain English. At the same time, I provided training for lawyers at the bank, so they could begin redrafting the bank's basic deposit agreement into plain English. One of the senior attorneys at the bank, after completing the training, set up Microsoft Word to assess her average sentence length, Flesch Reading Ease score, and Flesch–Kincaid grade level. She then began to redraft a 14-page section of the deposit agreement into plain English.

The original text had the following traits:

- Average sentence length: 42 words
- Flesch Reading Ease score: 27 ("very difficult," according to Flesch)
- Flesch–Kincaid grade level: 19

Notice the grade level: that's the level for a lawyer, and the score suggests that the document was really written for lawyers.

The lawyer also assessed one other aspect of the document. The readability statistics Microsoft Word provides include the percentage of passive-voice sentences. (Microsoft Word does a good job of identifying passive voice.) The original had 50 percent passive-voice sentences. The lawyer knew what we discussed in Chapter 9—that excessive passive voice is a recurring problem in legal drafting and can make legal writing dry, formal, and unnecessarily complex. After she completed a rewrite of the 14 pages, applying the principles I suggested (which are the principles in this book), she reassessed those four aspects of the text. Here's what she found:

- Average sentence length: 22 words
- Flesch Reading Ease score: 57
- Flesch–Kincaid grade level: 9
- Passive-voice sentences: 20 percent

Of course, the revised text might have been nonsensical gibberish. But probably not. That's the job of a lawyer: make the text sensible and grammatically correct. Assuming you've done those jobs, the numerical scores are a good indicator of how difficult a nonlegal reader would find the text (or how easy).

Because word processors are not sophisticated human readers, their judgments about the readability of a piece of text are naturally limited. For example, if your document contains many legal citations, these will be construed as single or even multiple sentences, and they will inflate the Flesch score and push the average sentence length down. Keep that in mind. If your text contains topic headings, tabulated lists, and extensive numbering, you may again see your average sentence length drop artificially and your readability score rise artificially.

Thus, readability scales are useful but rough assessments that give you a numerical measure. They're tools. They help. But you shouldn't let yourself become fixated on them.

Some examples

Here are some before-and-after examples with their numerical assessments.

Original jury instructions

Do not conceal information or give answers which are not true. Listen to the questions and give full and complete answers.

Do not make personal inspections, observations, investigations, or experiments nor personally view premises, things or articles not produced in court.

If you do not obey the instructions I am about to give you, it may become necessary for another jury to re-try this case with all of the attendant waste of your time here and the expense to the litigants and the taxpayers of this county for another trial.

We shall try the case as fast as possible consistent with justice, which requires a careful and correct trial.

- Average sentence length: 22 words
- Flesch Reading Ease score: 50
- Flesch–Kincaid grade level: 12

Revised jury instructions

Be honest when the lawyers ask you questions, and always give complete answers.

Do not view or inspect places or items from this case unless they are presented as evidence in court.

If you do not follow these instructions, I may have to order a new trial and start this process over again. That would be a waste of time and money, so please listen carefully to these instructions.

I assure you we will handle this case as fast as we can, but we cannot rush things. We have to do it fairly, and we have to follow the law.

- Average sentence length: 16 words
- Flesch Reading Ease score: 77
- Flesch–Kincaid grade level: 7

Original disclaimer

The holder is admitted on condition, and by use of this ticket agrees, that he will not transmit or aid in transmitting any description, account, picture or reproduction of the baseball game or exhibition to which this ticket admits him. Breach of the foregoing will automatically terminate this license.

The holder assumes all risk and dangers incidental to the game of baseball including specifically (but not exclusively) the danger of being injured by thrown or batted balls and agrees that the participating clubs, their agents and players are not liable for injuries resulting from such causes. The management reserves the right to revoke the license granted by this ticket.

- Average sentence length: 27 words
- Flesch Reading Ease score: 34 ("fairly difficult," according to Flesch)
- Flesch–Kincaid grade level: 15

Revised disclaimer

This ticket admits you to the event listed on the front. By using it, you agree not to broadcast or help broadcast any descriptions or pictures of the event. If you do, you must leave the event.

By using this ticket, you accept the risks of attending a baseball game. For example, you could be hit by thrown or batted balls or injured in other ways. Stadium management, its representatives, the teams, and the players are not responsible for those injuries.

Management can revoke this ticket and remove you from the event.

- Average sentence length: 13 words
- Flesch Reading Ease score: 64

- Flesch–Kincaid grade level: 7

If you've never used the Flesch Reading Ease score or the Flesch–Kincaid grade level, you should try them. For all your legal writing, particularly writing aimed at nonlawyers, these numerical assessments can give you a sense of your effectiveness. Just remember that they're only tools.

For a thorough understanding of the Flesch Reading Ease score, you should read Rudolf Flesch's book *How to Write Plain English: A Book for Lawyers and Consumers*.

Before and After

1. Before

WHEREAS, Attorney is about to undertake the performance of substantial legal services on behalf of the Personal Representative; and

WHEREAS, the State Bar's rules of professional conduct encourage attorneys and clients to enter into fee agreements; and

WHEREAS, the Probate Code requires that attorney fee agreements be signed by the personal representative;

NOW THEREFORE, in consideration of their mutual promises stated herein, the parties hereby agree that: ...

1. After

The Attorney is about to perform substantial legal services for the Personal Representative.

The State Bar's rules of professional conduct encourage attorneys and clients to have fee agreements.

The Probate Code requires that attorney-fee agreements be signed by the Personal Representative.

Therefore, the parties agree as follows: ...

2. Before

This publishing contract is entered by Jackie Griffin (hereinafter "Griffin") and Evermore Computer Publishing House, Inc. (hereinafter "ECPHI").

126 Plain Legal Writing: Do It

2. After

Parties to the Publishing Contract

Jackie Griffin
3348 Metz Lane
Marlton, NJ 08053

Evermore Computer Publishing House, Inc.
2899 Worthington Drive
Grand Prairie, NJ 08050

Background

Griffin and Evermore have agreed that Griffin will write and Evermore will publish a book aimed at the technology market....

3. Before

THE HOLDER IS ADMITTED ON CONDITION, AND BY USE OF THIS TICKET AGREES, THAT HE WILL NOT TRANSMIT OR AID IN TRANSMITTING ANY DESCRIPTION, ACCOUNT, PICTURE OR REPRODUCTION OF THE BASEBALL GAME OR EXHIBITION TO WHICH THIS TICKET ADMITS HIM. BREACH OF THE FOREGOING WILL AUTOMATICALLY TERMINATE THIS LICENSE.

THE HOLDER ASSUMES ALL RISK AND DANGERS INCIDENTAL TO THE GAME OF BASEBALL INCLUDING SPECIFICALLY (BUT NOT EXCLUSIVELY) THE DANGER OF BEING INJURED BY THROWN OR BATTED BALLS AND AGREES THAT THE PARTICIPATING CLUBS, THEIR AGENTS AND PLAYERS ARE NOT LIABLE FOR INJURIES RESULTING FROM SUCH CAUSES. THE MANAGEMENT RESERVES THE RIGHT TO REVOKE THE LICENSE GRANTED BY THIS TICKET.

3. After

This ticket admits you to the event listed on the front. By using it, you agree not to broadcast or help broadcast any descriptions or pictures of the event. If you do, you must leave the event.

By using this ticket, you accept the risks of attending a baseball game. For example, you could be hit by thrown or batted balls or injured in other ways. Stadium management, its representatives, the teams, and the players are not responsible for your injuries.

Management can revoke this ticket and remove you from the event.

4. Before

TO: ALL RECORD AND BENEFICIAL HOLDERS OF THE COMMON STOCK OF ETRA, INC. (THE "COMPANY"), INCLUDING ALL OF ITS PREDECESSORS, DURING THE PERIOD BEGINNING ON AND INCLUDING JANUARY 1, 1995 THROUGH AND INCLUDING MARCH 22, 2007.

PLEASE READ THIS NOTICE CAREFULLY AND IN ITS ENTIRETY. YOUR RIGHTS MAY BE AFFECTED BY THE LEGAL PROCEEDINGS IN THIS LITIGATION. BROKERAGE FIRMS, BANKS, AND OTHER PERSONS OR ENTITIES WHO ARE MEMBERS OF THE CLASS IN THEIR CAPACITIES AS RECORD OWNERS, BUT NOT AS BENEFICIAL OWNERS, ARE DIRECTED TO SEND THIS NOTICE PROMPTLY TO BENEFICIAL OWNERS.

The purpose of the notice is to inform you of this lawsuit (the "Action"), a proposed settlement of the Action (the "Settlement"), and a hearing to be held by the Circuit Court (the "Court"), on October 5, 2007, at 1 p.m. (the "Settlement Hearing"), at which the Court shall consider for approval: (i) whether this Action will be certified as a class action, for settlement purposes only, pursuant to Rule of Civil Procedure 23; (ii) whether the terms and conditions of the Settlement are fair, reasonable, adequate, and in the best interests of the Class and the Company; (iii) whether the Final Order should be entered dismissing this Action with prejudice as against Plaintiffs and the Class, releasing the Settled Claims, and enjoining prosecution of any and all Settled Claims; (iv) the award of Plaintiffs' counsel's attorneys' fees and expenses as provided for herein, as to which award Company has agreed to pay $7.5 million; (v) any objections to the Settlement; and (vi) such other relief as the Court may deem necessary and appropriate. Any of the dates set forth herein may be modified by the Court without further notice. The Court reserves the right to approve the Settlement at or after the Settlement Hearing with such modifications as may be consented to by the parties to the Stipulation and without further notice to the Class.

THE DESCRIPTION OF THE ACTION AND THE SETTLEMENT WHICH FOLLOWS HAS BEEN PREPARED BY COUNSEL FOR THE PARTIES. THE COURT HAS MADE NO FINDING WITH RESPECT TO SUCH MATTERS, AND THIS NOTICE IS NOT AN EXPRESSION OR STATEMENT BY THE COURT OF FINDINGS OF FACT.

4. After

If you owned stock in Etra, Inc. between January 1, 1995, and March 22, 2007, you may have rights in a class-action lawsuit.

- Read this notice carefully—it affects your rights.
- Brokers and agents: forward this notice to beneficial owners of Etra stock.

This class-action lawsuit might be settled. This notice explains the details and how you can participate if you want to.

The judge will hold a hearing about the settlement on October 5, 2007. At the hearing, the judge will consider these things:

- whether to dismiss this lawsuit and prevent the plaintiffs from suing again;
- whether to approve this lawsuit as a class action;
- whether the settlement is fair, reasonable, adequate, and in the best interests of the class and Etra;
- whether there are any objections to the settlement;
- whether to give the plaintiffs' lawyers $7.5 million in fees and expenses—which Etra has agreed to pay;
- anything else the judge thinks is appropriate.

The judge can change the date without notice, and the judge can approve the settlement at the hearing or later. If the parties agree, the judge can change the details of the settlement without notice to the class.

The lawyers prepared this document, not the judge.

The judge has not made any decisions yet.

5. Before

KNOW ALL MEN BY THESE PRESENTS, that I/we Linda Smith residing at 1000 Amber Lane, Emmett, ID, the undersigned, First Party, for and in consideration of the sum of FIVE THOUSAND AND NO/100 Dollars ($5,000.00) to me/us in hand paid by Real Insurance, Inc. and John James, Second Party, the receipt of which is hereby acknowledge, I/we being of lawful age, for myself/ourselves, my/our heirs, administrators, executors, successors and assigns hereby remise, release, acquit and forever discharge the said Second Party, his/her, their, and each of their heirs, executors, administrators, successors, and assigns and any and all other persons, partnerships, associations, and/or corporations, whether herein named or referred to or not, of and from any and every claim, demand, right, or cause of action of whatever kind and nature, either in law or equity, especially liability arising from an accident which occurred on or about 08/11/2005 at or near the following location INTERSTATE 84, CALDWELL, IDAHO, USA for which I/we have claimed the said Second Party to be legally liable, but this release shall not be construed as an admission of liability.

5. After

Form to release your claims

Us:	Real Insurance, Inc.	You:	Linda Smith
	250 Gray St. #500		1000 Amber Lane
	Boise, ID 83706		Emmett, ID 83770

Our insured: John James

By signing this release form, you give up all your claims against us and against our insured. In return, we'll pay you $5,000. The claims you're giving up are from an accident on August, 11, 2005, near Interstate 84, Caldwell, ID. We and our insured admit no liability.

You're giving up all your claims against us and any other person or company related to us. You're giving up all your claims for anyone else who might act for you or who might have rights through you.

6. Before

Player also shall reimburse Contract Advisor for all reasonable and necessary travel expenses actually incurred by Contract Advisor during the term hereof in the negotiation of Player's NFL contract, but only if such expenses and approximate amounts thereof shall be approved in advance by Player.

...

In performing these services, Contract Advisor acknowledges that he/she is acting in a fiduciary capacity on behalf of Player and agrees to act in such manner as to protect the best interests of Player and assure effective representation of Player in individual contract negotiations ...

6. After

You agree to reimburse the Contract Advisor for all reasonable and necessary travel expenses the Contract Advisor incurs—related to negotiating your NFL contract—during the term of this agreement. The Contract Advisor must get your approval for the approximate amounts of those expenses in advance.

...

In performing these services, the Contract Advisor is acting in a fiduciary capacity—meaning with the utmost good faith—for you. The Contract Advisor agrees to protect your best interests and to represent you effectively in negotiating your NFL contract.

7. Before

Attorney is about to undertake the performance of substantial legal services on behalf of the Personal Representative, for which Attorney shall be paid fees and costs. The Personal Representative has retained Attorney to provide legal services to the Personal Representative for administration of the probate estate.

7. After

I'm about to begin doing important legal work for you. You've hired me to represent you in administering the probate estate. You'll be paying my fees and costs.

8. Before

Therapeutic Recovery Care Hospital for Children ("TRCHC") has provided this web site for educational and informational purposes only. The material contained herein is believed to be complete and generally in accord with accepted standards at the time of publication. However, because of the possibility of human error and changes in medical science, TRCHC and its employees do not warrant that the information contained herein is in every respect accurate or complete, and thus, are not responsible for any errors or omissions or for the results obtained from the use of such information. TRCHC makes no representation or warranties, expressed or implied, and disclaims any liability for injury and any other damages which result from an individual using techniques discussed on this site.

8. After

We (the Therapeutic Recovery Care Hospital for Children and its employees) provide this website for education and information only. We believe the material here is complete and generally met accepted standards when we published it. But because people make mistakes and medical science changes, we don't promise (or warrant) that the information is entirely accurate or complete. We aren't responsible for any errors or omissions or for the results if you use this information. We make no representations or warranties, expressed or implied, and we're not liable for injury or any other damages if you use techniques discussed on this site.

9. Before

Do not conceal information or give answers which are not true. Listen to the questions and give full and complete answers.

132 Plain Legal Writing: Do It

Do not make personal inspections, observations, investigations, or experiments nor personally view premises, things or articles not produced in court.

If you do not obey the instructions I am about to give you, it may become necessary for another jury to re-try this case with all of the attendant waste of your time here and the expense to the litigants and the taxpayers of this county for another trial.

We shall try the case as fast as possible consistent with justice, which requires a careful and correct trial.

...

You are instructed that you may not draw an adverse inference from the witness's claim of privilege.

9. After

Be honest when the lawyers ask you questions, and always give complete answers.

Do not view or inspect places or items from this case unless they are presented as evidence in court.

If you don't follow these instructions, I may have to order a new trial and start this process over again. That would be a waste of time and money, so please listen carefully to these instructions.

I assure you we will handle this case as fast as we can, but we can't rush things. We have to do it fairly, and we have to follow the law.

...

A privilege is the right not to testify. Do not assume anything when a witness uses a privilege.

10. Before

Reproduction of all or part of the contents of this page in any form is prohibited other than for individual use and it may not be recopied and shared with a third party. The permission to recopy by an individual does not allow for incorporation of this material or any part of it in any work or publication, whether in hard copy, electronic, or any other form.

10. After

You may not copy all or part of the contents of this page in any form—other than for individual use—and you may not share it with anyone else. If we permit you to copy, you may not put this material or any part of it into any work or publication, whether in hard copy, electronic, or any other form.

11. Before

"Cash" means cash, cash equivalents, other short term investments having a readily ascertainable market value, investments held in board designated funds, excluding, however, any such assets whose use is limited to payment of current liabilities, all Trustee held funds, and malpractice funds.

11. After

"Cash" means

(a) cash;

(b) cash equivalents;

(c) other short-term investments with a readily ascertainable market value;

(d) assets held in board-designated funds, but not any of those assets whose use is limited to paying current liabilities;

(e) all Trustee-held funds; and

(f) malpractice funds.

12. Before

On January 31, 2005, WyTech Sales, Inc. (the "Borrower") entered into an agreement with Nuttall Systems & Technology Transfer, Inc. ("NSTT") under which all of the Borrower's accounts receivable ("Receivables") of which you are the obligor have been pledged to NSTT. The Borrower has established a lockbox (the "Lockbox") for collection of Receivables. Accordingly, you are hereby instructed to remit all payments of Receivables of which you are, or have been, the obligor to ...

12. After

Beginning January 31, 2005, please pay accounts you owe to WyTech Sales, Inc. to Nuttall Systems & Technology Transfer, Inc. instead. This letter explains how.

Background. On January 31, 2005, WyTech Sales, Inc., the borrower, gave Nuttall Systems all its accounts receivable as collateral. You are the payer on some of those accounts. So from now on, pay those accounts to Nuttall Systems through a lockbox the borrower has established here: ...

13. Before

THIS PARKING PASS IS A REVOCABLE LICENSE THAT LICENSES THE HOLDER TO PARK 1 VEHICLE IN 1 PARKING SPOT AT CHERRY PARK CENTER ("CPC"), AT HOLDER'S SOLE RISK. HALL CHERRY PARK LLC, REGAN HOCKEY CLUB, THE CITY OF CHERRY PARK AND EACH OF THEIR RESPECTIVE AFFILIATES, OWNERS, AGENTS AND EMPLOYEES (COLLECTIVELY, "HCP") ASSUME NO RESPONSIBILITY FOR THEFT OR DAMAGE TO THE VEHICLE OR ANY ARTICLE LEFT IN THE VEHICLE. HOLDER HEREBY AGREES THAT HPC IS NOT LIABLE FOR INJURIES OR DAMAGES RELATED TO HOLDER'S ATTENDANCE AT SUCH GAME OR EVENT OR THE PARKING OF THE VEHICLE. HCP ASSUMES NO RESPONSIBILITY FOR LOST, STOLEN OR DESTROYED PARKING PASSES. HOLDER IS NOT ENTITLED TO A CASH REFUND OR REPLACEMENT TICKET. THIS PASS DOES NOT CREATE AN EXPRESS OR IMPLIED BAILMENT AGREEMENT.

13. After

This parking pass allows you to park 1 vehicle in 1 parking spot at the Cherry Park Center.
- You park here at your own risk.
- We're not responsible for theft or damage to the vehicle or anything left in the vehicle (in legal terms, this pass doesn't create a bailment).

- We're not responsible for lost, stolen, or destroyed parking passes.
- You're not entitled to a cash refund or replacement pass.
- We can revoke the pass at any time.

While you're attending a game or event at Cherry Park Center, we're not responsible for injury or damage at the game or event.

"We" means Hall Cherry Park LLC, Regan Hockey Club, the City of Cherry Park, and each of their affiliates, owners, agents, and employees.

14. Before

INTEREST RATE AND LOAN FEE POLICY
(PRICING PACKAGE)

Lender Applicant(s) Occupancy: Loan Number Primary Secondary Investment Property Address	Term (in months) Purchase Refinance Other: _____ Loan Type: Fixed Rate Terms: ARM Loan Terms:	Interest Rate _____% Loan Fee _____% Discount Points _____% Initial Interest Rate _____% Loan Fee _____% Discount Points _____% Margin _____% Lifetime Ceiling Rate Cap _____%

14. After

Interest Rate and Loan Fee Policy
Pricing Package Agreement

This agreement allows you to lock in the interest rate (and other terms) for your loan, so you can know what interest rate you'll pay at closing, and you can avoid the risk that rates might rise. The items you lock in are called your Pricing Package.

This document has 4 parts:
1. Locking in your Pricing Package
2. Terms that apply to all loans
3. Reduced-documentation loans
4. Information about prepayment and other fees

15. Before

You have requested this firm provide Great Mountain Homeowners Association, Inc. (the "Association") with a legal opinion regarding whether Section 4.02 of the Association's Bylaws requires a candidate to receive a majority of the votes cast at an annual meeting in order to be properly elected to the Board of Directors.

...

15. After

You've asked us to give Great Mountain Homeowners Association a legal opinion on Section 4.02 of the Association's Bylaws. Specifically, for election to the Board of Directors, does Section 4.02 require a candidate to receive a majority of the votes cast at an annual meeting, or is it enough that the candidate received more votes than the next competing candidate?

Summary. Although long-standing Association practice has been to seat candidates who received more votes than the next competing candidate—and that practice may be legal—it would be safer to conduct a run-off election for the contested seat.

16. Before

<u>ATTORNEY'S HOURLY FEE AGREEMENT</u>

AGREEMENT made by and between the following persons: Personal Representative: Jade Hansen. Attorney: Andrew Decillo. Residuary Beneficiaries: Tyler and Meghan Hansen.

WITNESSETH

WHEREAS, Attorney shall undertake the performance of substantial legal services on behalf of the Personal Representative, for which Attorney shall be paid fees and costs; and

WHEREAS, the State Bar's Rules of Professional Conduct encourage attorneys and clients to enter into fee agreements at the commencement of representation in order to avoid the possibility of misunderstandings; and

WHEREAS, the State Probate Code requires that attorney fee agreements be signed by the Personal Representative and by the persons bearing the impact of the fees;

NOW THEREFORE, in consideration of their mutual promises stated herein, the parties hereby agree that:

The Personal Representative has retained Attorney to provide legal services to the Personal Representative for administration of the above probate estate at hourly rates of $175 for attorney time and $85 for paralegal time for all matters handled, including but not limited to ordinary services and extraordinary services.

Notwithstanding the foregoing, Attorney agrees not to bill fees for ordinary services of Attorney that would exceed the percentage fees provided for in State Statutes Section 733.6171.

Fees shall be billed by Attorney and paid by the Personal Representative out of the assets of the Estate on a monthly basis. Costs incurred for copies, postage, long distance, fax, FedEx, filing fees, and other items shall also be billed and paid at least monthly.

The parties agree that the provisions of this Fee Agreement replace the provisions of the applicable statutes and case law and that Attorney will not charge fees based upon a percentage of ordinary services by the attorney for the Personal Representative: $1,500 for the first $40,000 plus $750 for the next $30,000 plus $750 for the next $30,000 plus 3% of the rest of the inventory value and income of the probate estate for ordinary services. The statute also provides that the attorney, personal representative and persons bearing the impact of the compensation may agree to compensation determined in a different manner. The statute also provides that attorneys are entitled to additional compensation for extraordinary services, such as real estate, adversary proceedings, homestead, tax matters, business, etc.

If the matter of fees and costs is submitted to the Court for review or determination at any time, fees and costs shall be billed by and paid to Attorney for such fee proceeding on the same basis as other fees under this Agreement; i.e., billed and paid at least monthly. In addition, attorneys testifying as expert witnesses on the matter of fees shall be entitled to fees at their usual hourly rates, which shall be paid out of the estate.

The parties agree that Attorney represents Jade Hansen in his or her capacity as Personal Representative of the Estate and also in his or her capacity as Successor Trustee of THE HANSEN FAMILY TRUST. The parties understand the potential conflict of interest arising from representation of multiple parties in multiple roles. They understand that in the event that a conflict should ever develop between the multiple clients concerning the Estate or Trust, then Attorney would not be able to represent either of the clients in that conflict. The Personal Representative, Trustee and residuary beneficiaries are encouraged to engage his or her own separate lawyer before executing this agreement if they desire legal advice concerning this Fee Agreement or concerning any other aspect of the probate estate or Trust.

UNDER PENALTIES OF PERJURY, WE DECLARE THAT WE HAVE READ THE FOREGOING, AND THE FACTS ALLEGED ARE TRUE, TO THE BEST OF OUR KNOWLEDGE AND BELIEF.

Duly executed:

_____

16. After

Agreement to Administer the Estate of [Name] for an Hourly Fee

1. Parties

This agreement is between:

- Andrew Decillo, the attorney (I or me);
- Jade Hansen, the estate's personal representative (you); and
- Tyler and Meghan Hansen, the estate's residuary beneficiaries (the beneficiaries).

2. Background

You've asked me to administer the probate estate of [Name] in State. You're the personal representative. In administering that estate, I'll be performing a legal service for you, and you'll pay me for my time and expenses. You, the beneficiaries, and I are signing this fee agreement because (1) the State Bar encourages us to agree on a fee structure in writing and in advance to avoid misunderstandings, and (2) the Vermont Probate Code requires that attorney-fee agreements for estate administration be signed by representatives and estate beneficiaries.

3. Terms

I charge an hourly fee.

You'll pay me $175 per hour for attorney time and $85 per hour for paralegal time for all time my paralegals and I spend administering the estate.

There's a limit on my fee.

I won't bill you for ordinary services that exceed the percentages allowed by state law. But I can bill you for extraordinary services that exceed those limits.

I'll bill you monthly.

I'll bill you monthly for fees and expenses, and at that time you'll pay me from the estate's assets. I might bill you more often for some expenses, such as charges for copies, postage, telephone, and filing fees, and you'll pay those at that time from the estate's assets.

I won't be charging the statutory fees.

State law provides for default fees of—
- $1,500 for the first $40,000 of the estate,
- plus $750 for the next $30,000 of the estate,

- plus $750 for the next $30,000 of the estate,
- plus 3% of the remaining value of the estate for attorney services.

But the statute also allows us to agree to a different fee arrangement. The hourly fees in this agreement replace the default fees. I won't charge you based on a percentage of the value of the estate.

I'll charge you for going to court.

If a court has to review the fees and expenses for administering the estate, I'll bill you for the time and expense of that review process. If I have to call an attorney as an expert witness on fees during a court review, I'll bill you for that expense. You agree to pay these bills out of the estate.

This is a joint representation and could have conflicts of interest.

I represent you in your capacity as the personal representative of the estate and successor trustee of the [Name] trust. I also represent the beneficiaries. There's a potential conflict of interest when an attorney represents more than one party and a party in more than one role. If a conflict concerning the estate or the trust develops between you and the beneficiaries, then I won't be able to represent either you or the beneficiaries in that conflict. If you or the beneficiaries would like legal advice about this agreement, the estate, or the trust, then you and the beneficiaries should each hire a separate lawyer before signing this agreement.

Signed:

17. Before

I AM AWARE THAT IT IS THE POLICY OF THE STATE TO PROMOTE THE AMICABLE AND NONJUDICIAL SETTLEMENT OF DISPUTES INVOLVING CHILDREN AND FAMILIES. I AM AWARE OF ALTERNATIVE DISPUTE RESOLUTION METHODS, INCLUDING MEDIATION. WHILE I RECOGNIZE THAT ALTERNATIVE DISPUTE RESOLUTION IS AN ALTERNATIVE TO AND NOT A SUBSTITUTE FOR A TRIAL AND

THAT THIS CASE MAY BE TRIED IF IT IS NOT SETTLED, I REPRESENT TO THE COURT THAT I WILL ATTEMPT IN GOOD FAITH TO RESOLVE BEFORE FINAL TRIAL CONTESTED ISSUES IN THIS CASE BY ALTERNATIVE DISPUTE RESOLUTION WITHOUT THE NECESSITY OF COURT INTERVENTION.

17. After

By signing this statement, you affirm that:
- You know that the state promotes peaceful, out-of-court settlements of family-law cases.
- You know about non-court solutions, including mediation.
- You know that non-court solutions are an option and not a substitute for a trial.
- You know that this case may go to court if it is not settled.
- You promise to try—in good faith—to resolve this case out of court.